BLACK&DECKER®

HERE'S HOW...
TRIMWORK

24 Quick & Easy Makeovers for Walls, Windows & Doors

Creative Publishing
international

MINNEAPOLIS, MINNESOTA
www.creativepub.com

Contents

Introduction

Replacing or adding decorative moldings can renew your home like no other home improvement project. The materials are relatively inexpensive, compared to many home improvements, and the visual impact on your home can be priceless. For bargain-conscious homeowners, *Here's How: Trimwork* offers complete information on 24 important trimwork projects most popular with homeowners.

Unlike the larger, more expensive volumes, this book doesn't include the background information on woodworking skills and tools, and it doesn't offer the extensive catalog of the various materials available for trimwork. It also leaves out some project information that is of more interest to professionals than to homeowners. But *Here's How: Trimwork* does give you all the information you need to effectively make over your home's appearance with trim projects, some of which have traditional practicality, others featuring unique appeal. If you see yourself as a novice or even intermediate DIYer, this may well be the only book you'll need.

With *Here's How: Trimwork*, you'll learn the basics of installing all forms of wall molding, including baseboards, crown molding, chair rail, and picture rail. Also included are projects for trimming all kinds of doors and windows, including patio doors, basement egress windows, and French doors. A variety of decorative wall projects are found here, including several forms of wainscoting and tongue-and-groove paneling. Ceilings don't get left out either; you'll learn how to panel a ceiling and install creative architectural ceiling beams. There are even projects showing you how to create decorative wall shelves with ordinary stock moldings, and how to create a window shelf. A helpful appendix at the end of the book will teach you some basics on cutting and fitting joints with a power miter saw.

Today, it's hard to find a professional trim carpenter who'll charge you less than $1000 for an afternoon's worth of work. Armed with *Here's How: Trimwork*, though, you may very well save that thousand dollars on one project alone.

1. Installing One-piece Base Molding

Baseboard trim is installed to conceal the joint between the finished floor and the wallcovering (a necessary feature of a house). Installing plain, one-piece baseboard such as ranch-style base or cove base is a straightforward project. Outside corner joints are mitered, inside corners are coped, and long runs are joined with scarf cuts.

The biggest difficulty to installing base is dealing with out-of-plumb and nonsquare corners. However, a T-bevel makes these obstacles easy to overcome.

Plan the order of your installation prior to cutting any pieces and lay out a specific piece for each length of wall. It may be helpful to mark the type of cut on the back of each piece so you don't have any confusion during the install.

Locate all studs and mark them with painter's tape 6" higher than your molding height. If you need to make any scarf joints along a wall, make sure they fall on the center of a stud. Before you begin nailing trim in place, take the time to pre-finish the moldings. Doing so will minimize the clean-up afterward.

Baseboard doesn't need to be fancy to be effective. Without a shoe or a cap, a plain, one-piece base molding makes a neat transition from floor to wall.

Tools & Materials ▸

Pencil
Tape measure
Power miter saw

T-bevel
Coping saw
Metal file set

Pneumatic finish nail
 gun & compressor
Moldings

Pneumatic fasteners
Carpenter's glue
Finishing putty

How to Install One-piece Base Molding

Measure, cut, and install the first piece of baseboard. Butt both ends into the corners tightly. For longer lengths, it is a good idea to cut the piece slightly oversized (up to ¹⁄₁₆" on strips over 10 ft. long) and "spring" it into place. Nail the molding in place with two nails at every stud location.

Cut the second piece of molding oversized by 6" to 10" and cope-cut the adjoining end to the first piece. Fine-tune the cope with a metal file and sandpaper. Dry fit the joint adjusting it as necessary to produce a tight-fitting joint.

3

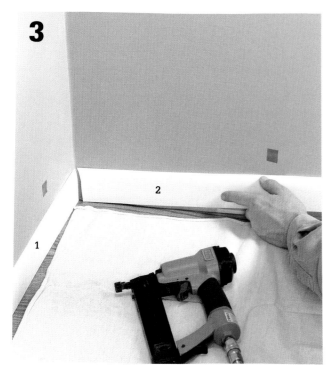

Check the corner for square with a framing square. If necessary, adjust the miter cut of your saw. Use a T-bevel to transfer the proper angle. Cut the second piece (coped) to length and install it with two nails at each stud location.

4

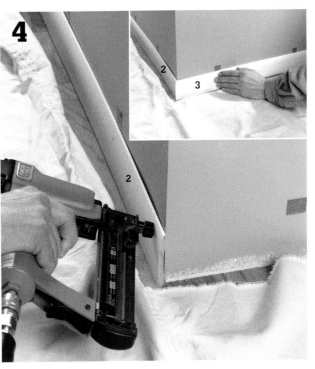

Adjust the miter angle of your saw to cut the adjoining outside corner piece. Test fit the cut to ensure a tight joint (inset photo). Remove the mating piece of trim and fasten the first piece for the outside corner joint.

5

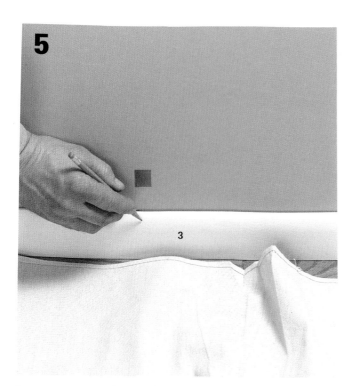

Lay out any scarf joints by placing the piece in position so that the previous joint is tight, and then marking the center of a stud location nearest the opposite end. Set the angle of your saw to a 30° angle and cut the molding at the marked location.

6

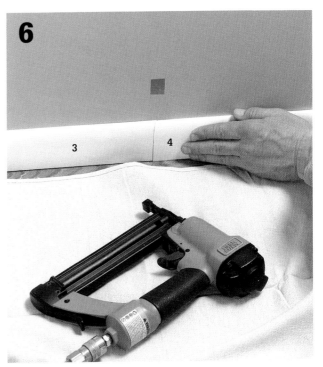

Nail the third piece in place, making sure the outside corner joint is tight. Cut the end of the fourth piece to match the scarf joint angle and nail it in place with two nails at each stud location. Add the remaining pieces of molding, fill the nail holes with putty, and apply a final coat of finish.

2. Installing a Built-up Base Molding

Built-up base molding is made up of several strips of wood (usually three) that are combined for a particular effect. It is installed in two common scenarios: to match existing trim in other rooms of a house; or to match a stock, one-piece molding that is not available.

Installing a built-up base molding is no more difficult than a standard one-piece molding, because the same installation techniques are used. However, built-up base molding offers a few advantages over standard stock moldings. Wavy floors and walls are easier to conceal, and the height of the molding is completely up to you, making heat registers and other obstructions easier to deal with.

In this project, the base molding is made of high-grade plywood rather than solid stock lumber. Plywood is more economical and dimensionally stable than solid lumber and can be built up to any depth, as well as cut down to any height. Keep in mind that plywood molding is less durable than solid wood, and is only available in 8 and 10-ft. lengths, making joints more frequent.

Tools & Materials ▸

Pneumatic finish nail gun
Air compressor
Air hose
Miter saw
Pencil
Tape measure
Hammer
Nail set
Table saw or straight edge guide
   and circular saw
Sandpaper
Power sander
¾" finish-grade oak plywood
Base shoe molding
Cap molding
2" finish nails
Wood putty

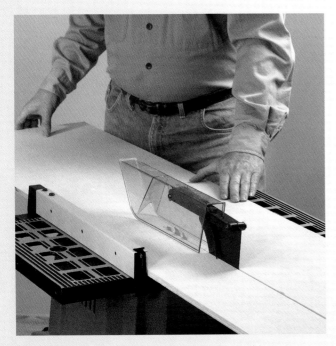

Cut the plywood panel into 6" strips with a table saw or a straightedge guide and a circular saw. Lightly sand the strips, removing any splinters left from the saw. Then, apply the finish of your choice to the moldings and the plywood strips.

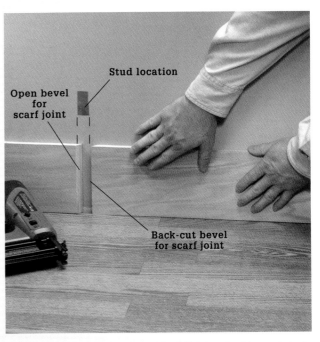

Install the plywood strips with 2" finish nails driven at stud locations. Use scarf joints on continuous runs, driving pairs of fasteners into the joints. Cut and install moldings so that all scarf joints fall at stud locations.

Tip ▶

Baseboard can be built up on the back with spacer strips so it will project further out from the wall. This can allow you to match existing casings, or to create the impression of a thicker molding. However, the cap rail needs to be thick enough to cover the plywood edge completely, or the core of the panel may be visible.

Installing a Built-up Base Molding

Nail and glue 45° outside miter joint before attaching baseboard

Test-fit inside corner butt joints before cutting a workpiece. If the walls are not square or straight, angle or bevel the end cut a few degrees to fit the profile of the adjoining piece. The cap molding will cover any gaps at the top of the joint. See illustration, page 8.

Miter outside corners squarely at 45°. Use wood glue and 1¼" brad nails to pull the mitered pieces tight, and then nail the base to the wall at stud locations with 2" finish nails. Small gaps at the bottom or top of the base molding will be covered with cap or base shoe.

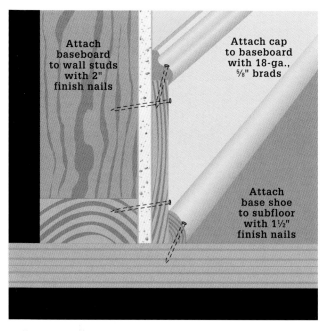

Attach baseboard to wall studs with 2" finish nails

Attach cap to baseboard with 18-ga., ⅝" brads

Attach base shoe to subfloor with 1½" finish nails

Use a brad nailer with 18-gauge, ⅝" brads to install the cap and base shoe moldings along the edges of the plywood base. Fit scarf joints on longer lengths, coped joints on inside corners, and miter joints on outside corners. Stagger the seams so that they do not line up with the base molding seams, following the suggested nailing pattern above. Set any protruding nails with a nail set and fill all nail holes with putty.

Built-up baseboard requires more attention to the nailing schedule than simple one-piece baseboards. The most important consideration (other than making sure your nails are all driven into studs or other solid wood), is that the base shoe must be attached to the floor, while the baseboard is attached to the wall. This way, as the gap between the wall and floor changes, the parts of the built-up molding can change with them.

Options with Heat Registers

Installing base molding around heat registers and cold-air returns can sometimes be challenging. Register thickness and height vary, complicating installation. Here are a few methods that can be employed for trimming around these obstructions.

Adjust the height of your base molding to completely surround the heat register opening, then cut a pocket out of the base for the heat register to slide into. Install the base shoe and cap trim molding continuously across the edges of the base molding.

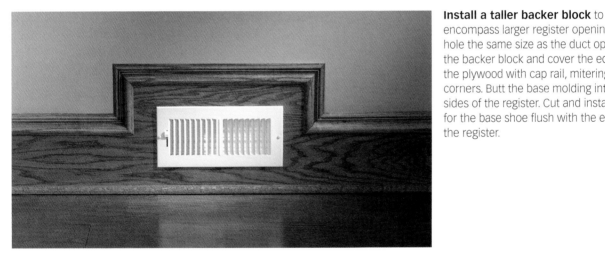

Install a taller backer block to encompass larger register openings. Cut a hole the same size as the duct opening in the backer block and cover the edges of the plywood with cap rail, mitering at the corners. Butt the base molding into the sides of the register. Cut and install returns for the base shoe flush with the ends of the register.

Install a wooden heat register for a less noticeable appearance. Wooden registers can be finished to match your trim and are available through most hardwood floor retailers. Butt the base molding into the ends of the register cover and bevel the front edges of the base shoe to match the depth of the register.

3. Installing Picture Rail

Picture rail molding is a specialty molding that was installed in many older homes so the homeowners could avoid making nail holes in the finished walls. Picture rail molding is a simple but elegant way to add style to any room. Special picture hanging hooks slide over the molding and artwork may be hung with a cord over the hook. Picture rail molding also provides its own decorative touch, breaking up the vertical lines from floor to ceiling. For this reason, it is also installed as a decorative touch by itself.

Picture rail molding is easy to install but should be reinforced with screws, not brads or nails, especially if you are hanging large, heavy items. Depending upon the style of your home, picture rail can be hung anywhere from 1 ft. to a few inches down from the ceiling. In some homes, picture rail is added just below the cornice or crown molding to add an additional layer of depth. When applied this way, it is commonly referred to as a frieze board.

In the example shown, the picture rail is installed using a level line to maintain height. If your ceiling is uneven, you may choose to install picture rail a set distance from the ceiling to avoid an uneven appearance.

Tools & Materials ▸

Ladder	4-ft. level
Pencil	or laser level
Stud finder	Drill with bits
Tape measure	Painter's tape
Power miter saw	Moldings
T-bevel	Pneumatic fasteners
Pneumatic finish nail	1⅝" wallboard screws
gun & compressor	Hole filler

How to Install Picture Rail Molding

Measure down the desired distance from the ceiling and draw a level reference line around the room using a pencil and a 4-ft. level (or, take advantage of modern technology and use a laser level). While you are up there, use a stud finder to locate the framing members, and mark the locations on the walls with blue painter's tape.

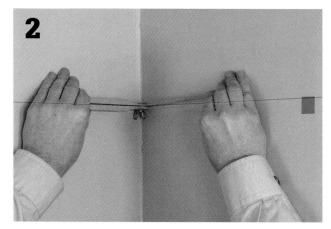

Use a T-bevel to measure the angle of the corner, tightening the lock nut with the blade and the handle on the reference line. Place the T-bevel on the table of your power miter saw and adjust the miter blade so that it matches the angle. See page 13.

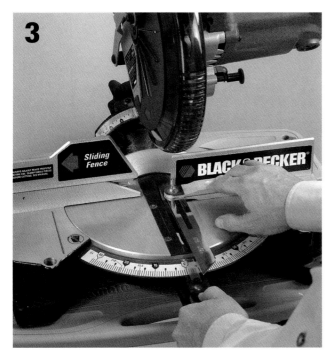

3

Most corners are close to 90°, but to cut a tight inside corner, the actual angle must be divided exactly in half. With the T-bevel tight to the fence, read the angle the saw is set to when it aligns with the T-bevel. If the blade is angled to the right of zero degrees the angle is larger than 90; to the left, smaller.

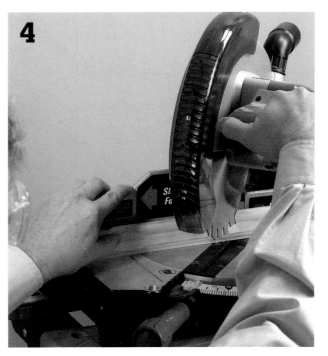

4

Read the angle from the miter saw table, divide the number by two, and add or subtract that number from 45 degrees to find the proper cutting angle for each corner. Cut each molding slightly longer than the measured length.

5

Nail the molding at the stud locations covering the level line around the room (if you're using a laser level, you simply keep it in position and turned on to cast a reference line you can follow). After each molding is completely nailed in place, go back to each stud location and drive 1⅝" wallboard screws into the molding through counter-bored pilot holes.

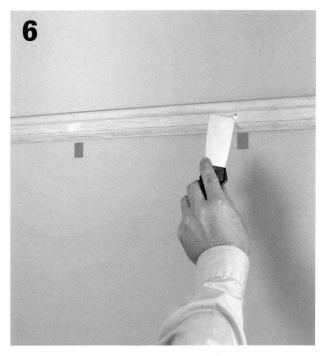

6

Fill nail holes with wood filler. Let the filler dry and sand it smooth. Then apply a final coat of paint over the molding face.

4. Installing Chair Rail

Chair rail molding typically runs horizontally along walls at a height of around 36" (the rule of thumb is to install it one-third of the way up the wall). Originally installed to protect walls from collisions with chair backs, today chair rail is commonly used to divide a wall visually. Chair rail may cap wainscoting, serve as a border for wallpaper, or divide two different colors on a wall. Or, more interesting chair rail profiles can be effective alone on a one-color wall.

Stock chair rail moldings are available at most lumberyards and home centers. However, more intricate and elaborate chair rails can be crated by combining multiple pieces of trim. Keep in mind the height of your existing furnishings when installing a chair rail. It is not good to find out that the new molding has a bad visual effect with your couch or chair backs when the project is completed.

Tools & Materials ▸

Pencil	Metal file set
Stud finder	Moldings
Tape measure	Pneumatic fasteners
Power miter saw	Painter's tape
4-ft. level	Carpenter's glue
Air compressor	Finishing putty
Finish nail gun	Finishing materials

Chair rail once was installed to protect fragile walls from chair backs, but today it is mainly installed as a decorative accent that breaks up dull walls visually.

How to Install Chair Rail

On the starting wall of your installation, measure up the desired height at which you plan to install the chair rail, minus the width of the molding. Mark a level line at this height around the room. Locate all studs along the walls and mark their locations with painter's tape below the line.

Measure, cut, and install the first piece of chair rail with the ends cut squarely, butting into both walls (in a wall run with two inside corners). Nail the molding in place with two 2" finish nails at each stud location.

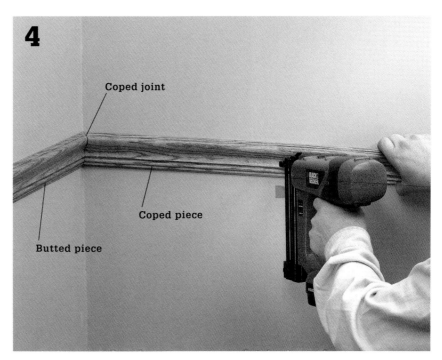

Miter-cut the second piece of molding with a power miter saw and then cope the end with a coping saw. Clean up the edge of the cope cut with a metal file to ensure a tight fit. Dry-fit the piece to check for any gaps in the joint.

Coped joint

Coped piece

Butted piece

When the coped joint fits tightly, measure, mark, and cut the opposing end of the second piece of trim squarely with a miter saw. Nail the second piece in place with two nails at each stud location. Follow the level line with the bottom edge of the molding.

Install the third piece of chair rail with a cope cut at one end. Use a butt joint where the molding runs into door and window casings. Fill all nail holes with putty and apply a final coat of finish to the molding.

Option: Cut a mitered return for the chair rail in areas where it will end without joining into another molding. Cut the return with a miter saw and glue it in place, using painter's tape to hold it until the glue dries.

5. Installing a Built-up Chair Rail

Designing and installing a built-up chair rail can be a very creative project that adds a considerable amount of style to any room. For the project shown, five smaller pieces of trim are combined with a 1×4 filler strip to create a bold, strong chair rail. If you are considering a larger built-up chair rail, make sure the existing base and crown moldings of the room will not be overshadowed. A good scale rule to remember is that chair rail should always be smaller than the crown or base.

If you plan to design your own molding, the choices are just about endless. It is a good idea to mimic the style of your existing moldings so that the new chair rail will not look out of place. If the room you are installing in currently has no chair rail, consider new wall finishes as well. Two-tone painted walls will emphasize the transition of a chair rail, as will changing the finish from paint to wallpaper or wainscoting.

Tools & Materials ▸

Ladder	4-ft. level
Pencil	or laser level
Stud finder	Painter's tape
Tape measure	Moldings
Power miter saw	Pneumatic fasteners
Coping saw	1⅝" wallboard sscrews
Pneumatic finish nail	Hole filler
gun & compressor	Finish materials
Drill with bits	

A built-up chair rail is made up of several styles of moldings, so the design options are virtually unlimited. The profile shown here features a strip of screen retainer on top of two pieces of profiled door stop. The stop molding is attached to a 1×4 filler that is then softened at the top and bottom edges with cover molding.

Choosing a Chair Rail Return

Before you begin installing the molding pieces of the built-up chair rail, decide what type of return you will use. Returns are finish details that occur in areas where different moldings meet at perpendicular angles, or quit in the middle of a wall. A beveled return (left) is a bit difficult to produce but has a clean look. On some built-up chair rail, you can take advantage of the depth of the molding by butting the back moldings up to the obstructions but running the cap moldings onto the surface (right).

How to Install a Built-Up Chair Rail

On the starting wall of your installation, mark the desired height of the first chair rail component you will install (here, the 1 × 4 filler strip). At this height, mark a level line around the room. Locate all studs along the walls and mark their locations with painter's tape above the line.

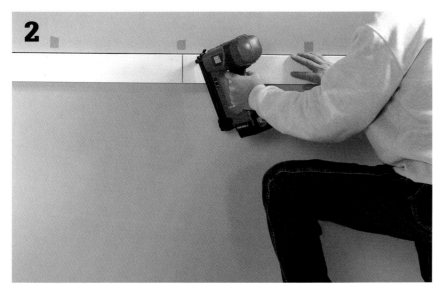

Cut and install the 1 × 4 filler strip so that the top edge of the strip follows the level line around the room. Fasten the strip with two, 2½" finish nails driven at every stud location. Butt the ends of the filler strip together, keeping in mind that the joints will be covered by additional moldings.

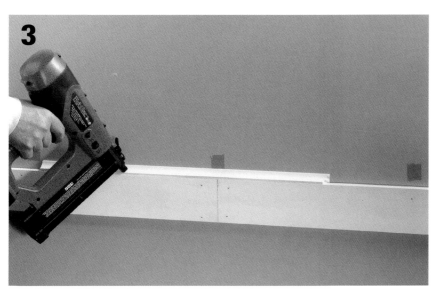

Cut and install the upper piece of cove molding around the room, nailing it flush to the top edge of the 1 × 4 filler strip. Use scarf joints on long runs, coped joints at inside corners and mitered joints on outside corners. Drive one nail at every stud location into the wall and one nail between each stud down into the filler strip.

(continued)

Install the lower piece of cove molding flush with the bottom edge of the filler strip. Use the same nailing sequence as with the upper cove molding. Cut scarf joints on long runs, coped joints at inside corners, and mitered joints on outside corners.

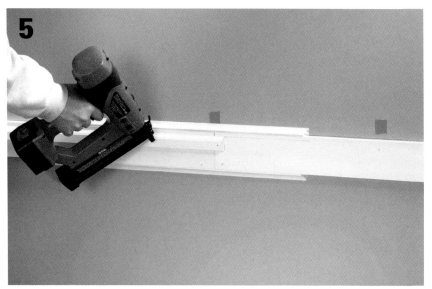

Measure, cut, and install the upper piece of stop molding around the room, driving two 2½" finish nails at each stud location. Cut scarf joints, coped joints, and mitered joints as necessary for each piece. Stagger the seams of the scarf joints on the stop molding so that they do not line up with the scarf joints of the cove moldings.

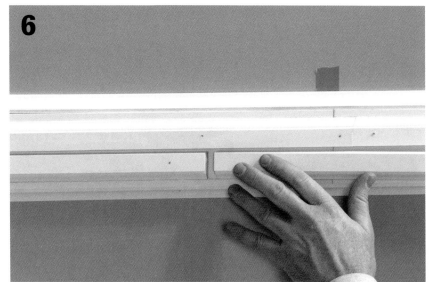

Install the lower piece of stop molding around the room, keeping the edge of the molding flush with the bottom edge of the filler strip. Fit each joint using the appropriate joinery method. Drive two nails at each stud location.

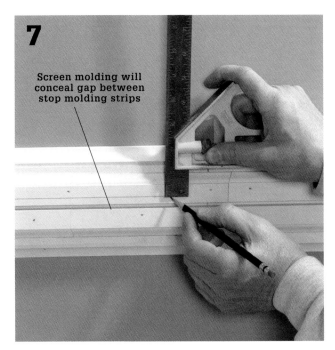

7

Screen molding will conceal gap between stop molding strips

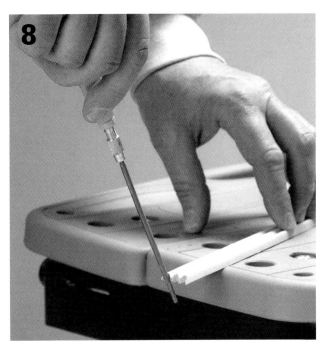

8

Set a combination square to 1⅜". Rest the body of the square on the top edge of the upper stop molding and use the blade of the square as a guide to mark a reference line around the room. This line represents the top edge of the screen molding.

Install the screen retainer molding, as with the other moldings, using the appropriate joints necessary. Fine-tune the cope cuts using a round metal file. Nail the molding in place with a brad nailer and 1⅝" brad nails. Keep the top edge of the molding flush with the reference line from step 7.

9

10

Set any nail heads with a nail set and fill all the nail holes with paintable wood filler. Check for any gaps in the joinery and fill them as well. Let the filler dry and sand it smooth with 180-grit sandpaper. Wipe the moldings with a dry cloth to remove any dust.

Use a paintbrush to apply a final coat of paint to the moldings. Cover the finished floor with a drop cloth and protect the lower portion of the wall from drips by masking it off with plastic if necessary.

6. Installing Basic Crown Molding

Simply put, crown molding is angled trim that bridges the joint between the ceiling and the wall. In order to cover this joint effectively, crown moldings are "sprung." This means that the top and bottom edges of the molding have been beveled, so when the molding is tilted away from the wall at an angle the tops and bottoms are flush on the wall and ceiling surfaces. Some crown moldings have a 45° angle at both the top and the bottom edges; another common style ("38° crown") has a 38° angle on one edge and a 52° angle on the other edge.

Installing crown molding can be a challenging and sometimes confusing process. Joints may be difficult for you to visualize before cutting, and wall and ceiling irregularities can be hard to overcome. If you have not worked on crown molding joints before, it is recommended that your first attempt be made with paint-grade materials. Stain-grade crown is commonly made of solid hardwood stock, which makes for expensive cutting errors, and difficulty concealing irregularities in joints.

Inside corner joints of crown molding should be cope cut, not mitered, except in the case of very intricate profile crown that is virtually impossible to cope (and must therefore be mitered). While mitering inside corners may appear to save time and produce adequate results, after a few changing seasons the joints will open up and be even more difficult to conceal.

Although many people install crown molding with nails driven directly into the ceiling and wall framing, irregularities in the surfaces are easier to overcome and adjustments are easier to make if the molding is nailed to a backing board. Backing boards or angled cleats are a convenient way to anchor crown molding without concern for stud or joist locations. They also eliminate the need for construction adhesive along the joint between the ceiling and the molding, on walls that are parallel with ceiling joists. Nailing the crown to a solid backer will allow you to hide many irregularities in the walls and ceiling, but not all of them. To fill gaps 1/8" or smaller use paintable caulk. To fill in gaps on clear-coat finishes, tape off the edge

Basic crown molding softens the transitions between walls and ceilings. If it is made from quality hardwood crown molding can be quite beautiful when installed and finished with a clear topcoat. But historically, it is most often painted—either the same color as the ceiling (your eye tends to see it as a ceiling molding, not a wall molding) or with highly elaborate painted and carved details.

of the molding with painter's tape and fill the gap with wallboard compound.

There are two methods to cutting crown molding on a power miter saw. The first is to hold the molding in a sprung position against the fence with the top edge of the molding against the saw table, or upside down. In this set-up, the position of the molding relative to the saw table and fence is the same as it will be relative to the wall and ceiling. This may sound difficult to do accurately, but with a 10" or a 12" saw it works quite well for basic crown moldings.

If you have a larger molding that does not fit under the blade of your saw in the sprung position, you'll need to cut this molding flat on the saw table with a compound saw. Many power miter saws have positive stops on both the miter and the bevel gauge that make it possible to cut crown molding at compound angles while it is lying flat on the saw table.

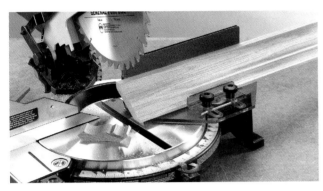

Cutting compound miters is tricky. Throughout this book, crown molding is shown being mitered with the workpiece held against a fence or fence extension. This hand-held approach is quick and effective, but takes some getting used to. A practically foolproof option is to use an adjustable jig, such as the compound miter jig shown here.

Tools & Materials ▶

Pencil	Nail set
Tape measure	Hammer
Circular saw	Metal files
Straightedge guide	2 × 4 material
Drill with bits	for backing
Coping saw	3" wallboard screws
Power miter saw	Carpenter's glue
Pneumatic finish	Crown molding, 2"
nail gun	1½" finish nails
Framing square	Fine-grit sandpaper
or combination	Hole filler
square	Paint and brushes

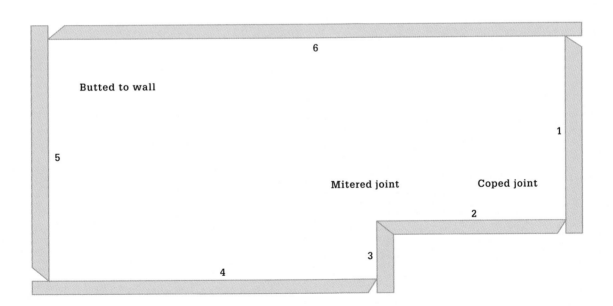

Plan the order of the installation to minimize the number of difficult joints on each piece and use the longest pieces for the most visible sections of wall. Notice that the left end of first piece is cope-cut rather than butted into the wall. Cope-cutting the first end eliminates the need to cope-cut both ends of the final piece, and places the cuts in the same direction. This simplifies your installation, making the method to cut each piece similar.

How to Use Backers to Install Crown Molding

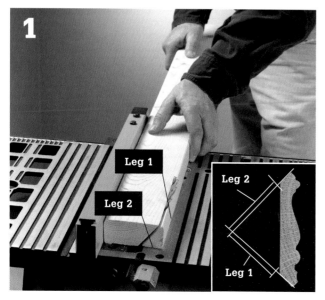

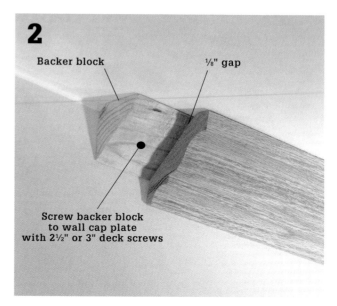

Installing crown molding is greatly simplified if you first attach triangular backers in the crotch area between the walls and ceilings. You can run the backers continuously along all walls or you can space them at regular intervals for use as nailers. To measure the required length for the triangle legs, set a piece of the crown molding in the sprung position in a square in an orientation like the inset photo above. Rip triangular backer strips from 2× stock on your table saw, with the blade set at 45°.

Locate the wall studs with a stud finder and mark the locations on the wall with blue painter's tape. Secure the backer block to the wall by driving 2½" or 3" deck screws at an angle through the block and into the top plate of the wall. Now, your crown molding can be attached to the backers wherever you'd like to nail it. Install crown according to the following instructions.

How to Install Basic Crown Molding

Cut a piece of crown molding about 1-ft. long with square ends. Temporarily install the piece in the corner of the last installation wall with two screws driven into the blocking. This piece serves as a template for the first cope cut on the first piece of molding.

Place the first piece of molding upside down and sprung against the fence of the miter saw. Mark a reference line on the fence for placement of future moldings, and cut the first coped end with an inside miter cut to reveal the profile of the piece.

3

Cope-cut the end of the first piece with a coping saw. Carefully cut along the profile, angling the saw as you cut to back-bevel the cope. Test-fit the coped cut against the temporary scrap from Step 1. Fine-tune the cut with files and fine-grit sandpaper.

4

Temporary scrap

Measure, cut to length, and install the first piece of crown molding, leaving the end near the temporary scrap loose for final fitting of the last piece. Nail the molding at the top and bottom of each stud location.

5

Test pieces

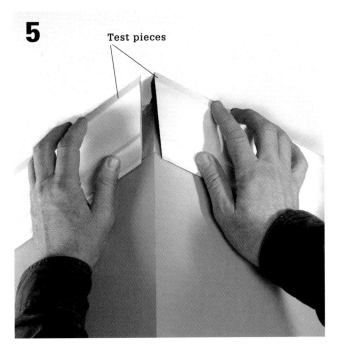

Cut two test pieces to check the fit of outside corners. Start with each molding cut at 45°, adjusting the angles larger or smaller until the joints are tight. Make sure the test moldings are properly aligned and are flush with the ceiling and walls. Make a note of your saw settings once the joint fits tightly.

6

Position the actual stock so a cut end is flush against the wall at one end and, at the other end, mark the outside corner on the back edge of the molding. Miter-cut the piece at the mark, according to the angles you noted on the test pieces.

(continued)

Measure and cut the third piece with an outside corner miter to match the angle of your test pieces. Cut the other end squarely, butting it into the corner. Install the piece with nails driven at stud locations. Install the subsequent pieces of crown molding, coping the front end and butting the other as you work around the room.

To fit the final piece, cope the end and cut it to length. Remove the temporary scrap piece from Step 3, and slide the last molding into position. Nail the last piece at the stud locations when the joints fit well, and finish nailing the first piece.

How to Make a Scarf Joint Using Crown Molding ▶

Use scarf joints when necessary, laying out the joint so it falls over a stud location. Keep the saw at the same angle to cut the second piece, and apply a bead of glue to the joint before nailing the molding in place.

Lightly sand the face of the scarf joint with fine-grit sandpaper to smooth out the face of the joint.

9

Fill all nail holes (use spackling compound if painting; wait until the finish is applied and fill with tinted putty for clear finishes). Use a putty knife to force spackling compound or tinted wood putty into loose joints and caulk gaps ⅛" or smaller between the molding and the wall or ceiling with flexible, paintable, latex caulk.

10

For gaps larger than ⅛" between the molding and the wall or ceiling, use a wallboard knife and compound to skim coat the wall and fill in the gap. Protect the finished surface of the molding with painter's tape.

11

Lightly sand the filled nail holes and joint gaps with fine sandpaper. Sand the nail hole flush with the surface of the moldings and apply a final coat of paint to the entire project.

7. Creating a Built-up Cornice

Designing your own cornice molding is a creative and fun process. A cornice is basically an elaborate crown molding, decorating the area where the wall meets the ceiling. Traditional cornices are made of plaster, one continuous solid molding piece, or a combination of simple molding pieces—called a built-up cornice. Built-up types are the most common today because the individual moldings are much cheaper and easier to install than one large piece. Built-up moldings also allow you to create a custom-designed molding that fits with the style of your room. To design your own cornice, visit a well-stocked lumberyard or home center and gather several molding samples of different types: baseboard, stop, crown, and bed moldings, as well as smaller trims, like quarter rounds and coves. Bring the samples home and arrange them in different combinations and positions to find the best design.

As you design your cornice, be careful not to overwhelm the room with a large, complicated molding. A good general rule is to try to match the size of the cornice to the overall size of your baseboard. Baseboard creates a visual balance with cornice when the two are proportionate.

Backing is another serious issue to consider when designing a built-up cornice. Whenever possible, install blocking inside the wall or ceiling. When blocking is not an option, consider using a backer block fastened directly to the wall studs as done in the project "Installing Basic Crown Molding" (page 20). A backer block allows you to firmly nail moldings in place when there are no joists in the ceiling to nail to. In the event you do not have framing or a blocking to nail to, use a bead of construction adhesive to adhere the molding to the ceiling and drive nails at opposing angles to hold the molding in place until the adhesive dries.

The cornice shown in this project starts with a $1\frac{3}{8}$" colonial stop installed along the ceiling, and a band of $3\frac{1}{2}$" baseboard run along the wall. A simple crown molding is then fastened to the two moldings to complete the cornice.

Tools & Materials ▸

Pencil	Hammer
Tape measure	Molding
Chalk line	2" and 1¼"
Power miter saw	finish nails
Pneumatic	Carpenter's glue
finish nailer	Construction
Nail set	adhesive

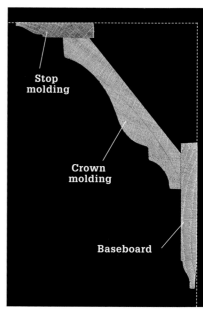

Stop molding

Crown molding

Baseboard

How to Create a Built-up Cornice

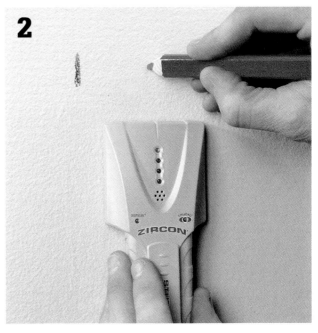

1

Cut a 4"- to 6"-long piece from each type of molding. Glue or nail the pieces together in the desired arrangement to create a marking template. Position the template flush with the wall and ceiling and mark along the outside edges of the ceiling and wall moldings. Mark at both ends of each wall.

2

Locate and mark all of the wall studs and ceiling joists, marking in areas that will be hidden by the crown molding.

3

Locate and mark all of the wall studs and ceiling joists, marking in areas that will be hidden by the crown molding. Snap chalk lines between the template marks you made in Step 2 (you can also mark with a pencil and level). If the ceiling has a deep texture, scrape off the texture just behind the chalk lines, using a drywall taping knife.

4

Install the ceiling trim, aligning its outside edge with the chalk line. Nail into the joists with 2" (6d) finish nails, and miter the joints at the inside and outside corners. Wherever possible, place the nails where they'll be hidden by the crown molding.

(continued)

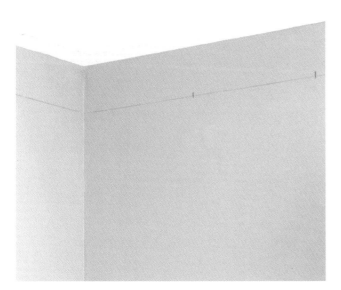

5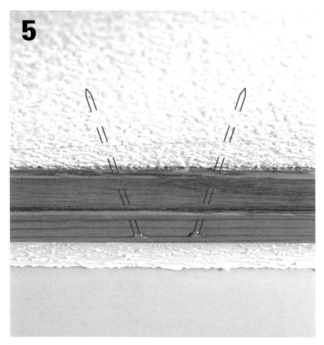

6

Where walls run parallel to the ceiling joists, and there are no joists to nail into, apply a bead of construction adhesive to the trim and nail it in place with pairs of nails driven at opposing angles. If you're handnailing, drill oversized pilot holes and secure the trim with coarse-thread drywall screws. Let the adhesive dry before starting the next step.

Install the vertical band trim along the walls, nailing into each stud with two 2" nails. Miter the band at outside corners.

7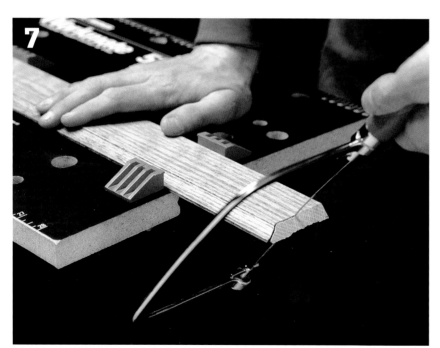

8

Cope the molding at inside corners by first cutting a 45° angle on the piece. Then cope-cut the angle with a coping saw. Cut along the front edge of the molding, following the contour. Test-fit the cut and fine-tune it with a metal file if necessary.

Add the crown molding, fastening it to the ceiling trim and wall band with 1¼" (3d) nails. Miter the molding at outside corners, and miter or cope the inside corners. Use a nail set to set all nails that aren't countersunk.

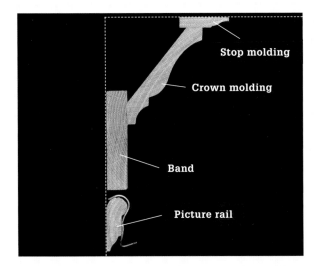

Stop molding

Crown molding

Band

Picture rail

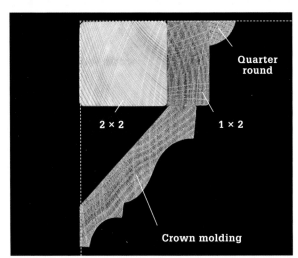

Quarter round

2 × 2

1 × 2

Crown molding

Use picture rail (page 12) to enhance a cornice molding. Standard height for picture rail is about 10" to 12" below the ceiling, but you can place it at any level. For a simple variation of the project shown, use square-edged stock for the band (since the bottom edge will mostly be hidden), and add picture rail just below the band. Be sure to leave enough room for placing picture hooks.

Install blocking to provide a nailing surface and added bulk to a built-up cornice. In this simple arrangement, a 2 × 2 block, or nailing strip, is screwed to the wall studs. A facing made from 1 × 2 finish lumber is nailed to the blocking and is trimmed along the ceiling with quarter-round. The crown molding is nailed to the wall studs along the bottom and to the nailer along the top.

This highly detailed Victorian-style built-up cornice is made up of several pieces of stock trim and solid stock ripped down to different widths. The right-angle component of this cornice may be screwed directly to the wall, to serve both a decorative function as well as serve as a nailer for the other trim elements. The screw holes are covered when the crown molding is installed.

Built up cornice treatments can be as simple or complex as you would like. This Arts & Crafts variation is made up of flat solid stock ripped down to specific dimensions. Two pieces of 1 × 2 stock are fastened together to form an "L" shaped angle. The angle is then screwed to the wall at the stud locations. An additional piece of 1" wide stock is nailed in place so the top edge is flush with the installed angle. This configuration creates a stepped cornice with a simpler appearance than the traditional sprung moldings. Notice that the "L" angle is nailed together with a slight gap at the back edge. This is done to compensate for irregularities in the corner joint.

8. Installing Polymer Crown Molding

Polymer moldings come in a variety of ornate, single-piece styles that offer easy installation and maintenance. The polystyrene or polyurethane material is as easy to cut as softwood, but unlike wood, the material won't shrink, and it can be repaired with vinyl spackling compound.

You can buy polymer moldings preprimed for painting, or you can stain it with a nonpenetrating heavy-body stain or gel. Most polymers come in 12-ft. lengths, and some have corner blocks that eliminate corner cuts. There are even flexible moldings for curved walls.

Tools & Materials ▸

Drill with
   countersink-
   piloting bit
Power miter saw or
   hand miter box
   and fine-tooth saw
Caulk gun
Putty knife
Crown molding

Finish nails
150-grit sandpaper
Rag
Mineral spirits
Polymer adhesive
2" drywall screws
Vinyl spackling
   compound
Paintable latex caulk

How to Install Polymer Crown Molding

Plan the layout of the molding pieces by measuring the walls of the room and making light pencil marks at the joint locations. For each piece that starts or ends at a corner, add 12" to 24" to compensate for waste. If possible, avoid pieces shorter than 36", because short pieces are more difficult to fit.

Hold a section of molding against the wall and ceiling in the finished position. Make light pencil marks on the wall every 12" along the bottom edge of the molding. Remove the molding, and tack a finish nail at each mark. The nails will hold the molding in place while the adhesive dries. If the wall surface is plaster, drill pilot holes for the nails.

WALL-MUR-MUUR   PARED-WAND-IL MURO

To make the miter cuts for the first corner, position the molding faceup in a miter box. Set the ceiling side of the molding against the horizontal table of the miter box, and set the wall side against the vertical back fence. Make the cut at 45°.

Check the uncut ends of each molding piece before installing it. Make sure mating pieces will butt together squarely in a tight joint. Cut all square ends at 90°, using a miter saw or hand miter box.

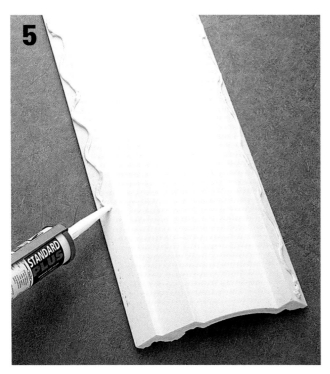

5

Lightly sand the backs of the molding that will contact the wall and ceiling, using 150-grit sandpaper. Slightly dampen a rag with mineral spirits, and wipe away the dust. Run a small bead of polymer adhesive (recommended or supplied by the manufacturer) along both sanded edges.

6

Set the molding in place with the mitered end tight to the corner and the bottom edge resting on the nails. Press along the molding edges to create a good bond. At each end of the piece, drive 2" drywall screws through countersunk pilot holes through the flats and into the ceiling and wall.

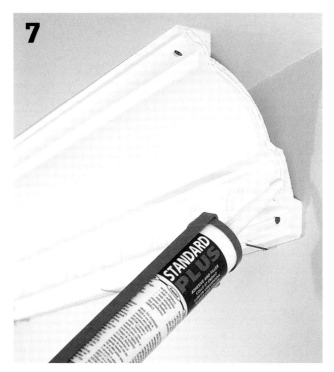

7

Cut, sand, and glue the next piece of molding. Apply a bead of adhesive to the end where the installed molding will meet the new piece. Install the new piece, and secure the ends with screws, making sure the ends are joined properly. Install the remaining molding pieces, and let the adhesive dry.

8

Carefully remove the finish nails and fill the nail holes with vinyl spackling compound. Fill the screw holes in the molding and any gaps in the joints with paintable latex caulk or filler, and wipe away excess caulk with a damp cloth or a wet finger. Smooth the caulk over the holes so it's flush with the surface.

9. Installing Crown Molding Lighting

Flexible, low-voltage rope lights hidden above a crown molding create a soft, comforting light effect that is much more relaxing than direct lighting. When combined with light-colored walls and ceilings, this system provides cool, balanced lighting, with no eye-straining glare. A stand-alone run along a wall can be used to draw attention to a room's focal point.

Rope lights can be easily adapted to any length of lighting run. Connect one rope to another by simply removing the end caps and inserting male/female connectors into the ends. You can also trim rope lighting to length at marked cutting lines located every 18".

Tools & Materials ▸

Stud finder
Pencil
Chalk line
Drill
Tape measure
Bevel gauge
Table saw
    or circular saw
Miter saw
Square
Jigsaw

Hammer
Nail set
Crown molding
Rope lighting
2 × 2 lumber
3" wallboard screws
6d finish nails
Mounting clips for
    rope lighting
    (optional)

How to Install Crown Molding Lighting

Use a stud finder to locate studs in the installation area. Mark the stud locations with light pencil marks near the ceiling, making sure the lines will be visible when the trim is in place. Plan the layout order of the molding pieces so as to minimize cuts and avoid noticeable joints. Also keep in mind the location of the receptacle that you plan to plug the rope lighting into.

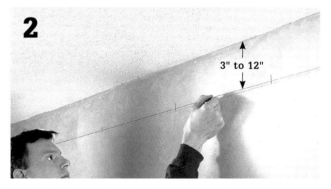

Determine the location for your molding. To maximize light reflection from the walls and ceiling, position the molding 3" to 12" from the ceiling. Measure from the ceiling and mark a point to represent the bottom edge of the molding. Mark at the ends of each wall that you plan to work on, then snap a chalk line between the marks.

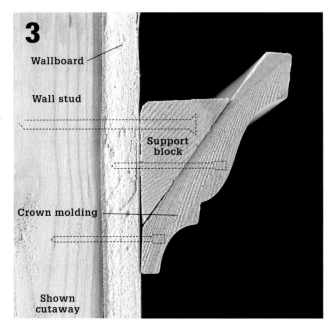

3

Wallboard

Wall stud

Support block

Crown molding

Shown cutaway

4

Because the crown molding will not be fastened at the top, it is necessary to install support blocking. Use a bevel gauge to determine the precise angle of your crown molding. Rip 2 × 2 lumber to this angle, using a table saw or circular saw. Fasten the supports to wall studs using 3" screws. The supports can be installed in long strips or cut into 6" blocks and attached at each molding joint and every 4 ft. on long runs of molding.

Set the molding in place along the chalk line. Have a helper hold the molding in place as you drill pilot holes and fasten it with 6d finish nails. Drive one nail into the stud along the lower edge of the molding and one into the support blocking. Use a nail set to recess the nail heads slightly.

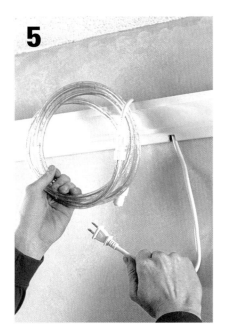

5

6

Install the remaining sections of molding. When you are above the receptacle you will use to power the rope lighting, cut a small notch in the molding with a jigsaw and lay the cord in the notch before fastening the molding to the wall.

Follow the manufacturer's instructions to join or cut any segments of rope lighting to the proper length. Lay the rope light in the trough between the wall and molding and work it around the entire installation. You may want to use mounting clips (sold separately) to keep the rope lighting lying flat. Plug in the light to activate it.

Variation: Flip the molding upside down and attach it to the wall for a cornice lighting effect. Attach the rope lighting to the top of the cornice with mounting clips sold separately by the manufacturer.

10. Casing a Window or Door

Stock wood casings provide an attractive border around window and door openings while covering the gaps between the wall surface and the window jamb. Install casings with a consistent reveal between the inside edges of the jambs and the edges of the casings.

In order to fit casings properly, the jambs and wall surfaces must be in the same plane. If one of them protrudes, the casing will not lie flush. To solve this problem, you may need to shave the edges of the jambs down with a block plane. Or you may need to attach jamb extensions to the window or door to match the plane of the wall. For small differences where a wallboard surface is too high, you can sometimes use a hammer to compress the wallboard around the jambs to allow the casings to lie flush.

Wallboard screws rely on the strength of untorn face paper to support the panel. If the paper around the screws becomes torn, drive additional screws nearby where the paper is still intact.

Tools & Materials ▸

Tape measure	Straightedge
Drill	Miter saw
Pencil	Casing material
Nail set	Baseboard molding
Hammer or	and corner blocks
pneumatic nailer	(optional)
Level	4d and 6d finish nails
Combination square	Wood putty

How to Install Mitered Casing on Windows & Doors

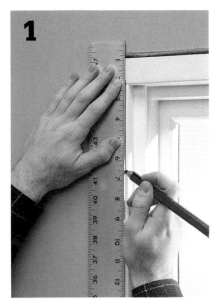

On each jamb, mark a reveal line ³⁄₁₆" to ¼" from the inside edge. The casings will be installed flush with these lines.

Place a length of casing along one side jamb, flush with the reveal line. At the top and bottom of the molding, mark the points where horizontal and vertical reveal lines meet. (When working with doors, mark the molding at the top only.)

Make 45° miter cuts on the ends of the moldings. Measure and cut the other vertical molding piece, using the same method.

Drill pilot holes spaced every 12" to prevent splitting, and attach the vertical casings with 4d finish nails driven through the casings and into the jambs. Drive 6d finish nails into the framing members near the outside edge of the casings.

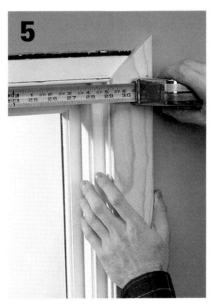

Measure the distance between the side casings and cut top and bottom casings to fit, with ends mitered at 45°. If window or door unit is not perfectly square, make test cuts on scrap pieces to find the correct angle of the joints. Drill pilot holes and attach with 4d and 6d finish nails.

Locknail the corner joints by drilling pilot holes and driving 4d finish nails through each corner, as shown. Drive all nail heads below the wood surface, using a nail set, then fill the nail holes with wood putty.

11. Installing Stool & Apron Window Trim

Stool and apron trim brings a traditional look to a window, and is most commonly used with double-hung styles. The stool serves as an interior sill; the apron (or the bottom casing) conceals the gap between the stool and the finished wall.

In many cases, such as with 2×6 walls, jamb extensions made from 1×2 finish-grade lumber need to be installed to bring the window jambs flush with the finished wall. Many window manufacturers also sell jamb extensions for their windows.

The stool is usually made from 1×2 finish-grade lumber, cut to fit the rough opening, with "horns" at each end extending along the wall for the side casings to butt against. The horns extend beyond the outer edge of the casing by the same amount that the front edge of the stool extends past the face of the casing, usually under 1".

If the edge of the stool is rounded, beveled, or otherwise decoratively routed, you can create a more finished appearance by returning the ends of the stool to hide the end grain. A pair of miter cuts at the rough horn will create the perfect cap piece for wrapping the grain of the front edge of the stool around the horn. The same can be done for an apron cut from a molded casing.

As with any trim project, tight joints are the secret to a successful stool and apron trim job. Take your time to ensure all the pieces fit tightly. Also, use a pneumatic nailer—you don't want to spend all that time shimming the jambs perfectly only to knock them out of position with one bad swing of a hammer.

Tip ▸

"Back-cut" the ends of casing pieces where needed to help create tight joints, using a sharp utility knife.

Tools & Materials ▸

Tape measure
Straightedge
Circular saw
  or jigsaw
Handsaw
Plane or rasp
Drill
Hammer

Pneumatic nailer
  (optional)
1 × finish lumber
Casing
Wood shims
4d, 6d, and 8d
  finish nails

How to Install Stool & Apron Window Trim

1

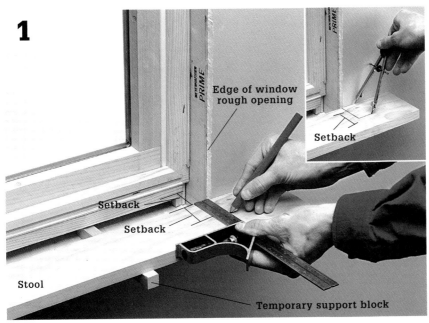

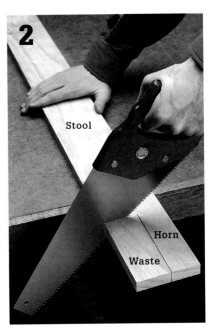

2

Cut the board for the stool to length, with several extra inches at each end for the horns. Temporarily position the stool in the window opening, pressed against the wall and centered on the window. Use a combination square to measure the setback distance from the window frame to the near edge of the stool. Mark the setback onto the stool at each edge of the window rough opening (if the measurements are different, use the greater setback distance for each end). Then, use a compass and pencil to scribe the profile of the wall onto the stool to complete the cutting line for the horn (inset photo).

Cut out the notches to create the stool horns. For straight lines, you can use a large handsaw, but for the scribed line use a more maneuverable saw like the jigsaw or a coping saw. Test-fit the stool, making any minor adjustments with a plane or a rasp so it fits tightly to the window frame and flush against the walls.

3

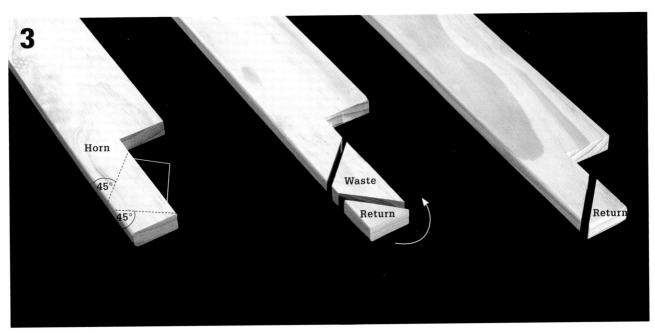

To create a return at the horn of the stool, miter-cut the return pieces at 45° angles. Mark the stool at its overall length and cut it to size with 45° miter cuts. Glue the return to the mitered end of the horn so the grain wraps around the corner. *Note: Use this same technique to create the returns on the apron, but make the cuts with the apron held on-edge, rather than flat.*

(continued)

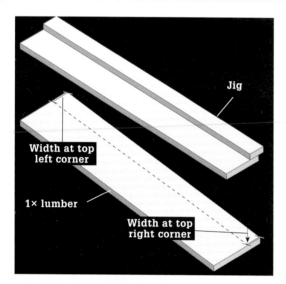

Where jamb extensions are needed, cut the head extension to its finished length—the distance between the window side jambs plus the thickness of both side extensions (typically 1× stock). For the width, measure the distance between the window jamb and the finished wall at each corner, then mark the measurements on the ends of the extension. Use a straightedge to draw a reference line connecting the points. Build a simple cutting jig, as shown.

Clamp the jig on the reference line, then rip the extension to width, using a circular saw; keep the baseplate tight against the jig and move the saw smoothly through the board. Reposition the clamp when you near the end of the cut. Cut both side extensions to length and width, using the same technique as for the head extension (see Tip).

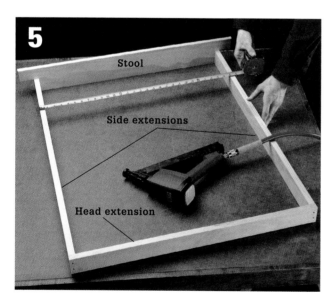

Build a box frame with the extensions and stool, using 6d finish nails and a pneumatic nailer. Measure to make sure the box has the same dimensions as the window jambs. Drive nails through the top of the head extension into the side extensions, and through the bottom of the stool into side extensions.

Apply wood glue to the back edge of the frame, then position it against the front edge of the window jambs. Use wood shims to adjust the frame, making sure the pieces are flush with the window jambs. Fasten the frame at each shim location, using 8d finish nails driven through pilot holes. Loosely pack insulation between the studs and the jambs, or use minimal-expanding spray foam.

7

Reveal mark

Reveal

8

Head casing

Stool

On the edge of each jamb or jamb extension, mark a 3/16" to 1/4" reveal. Place a length of casing along the head extension, aligned with the reveal marks at the corners. Mark where the reveal marks intersect, then make 45° miter cuts at each point. Reposition the casing at the head extension and attach, using 4d finish nails at the extensions, and 6d finish nails at the framing members.

Cut the side casings to rough length, leaving the ends slightly long for final trimming. Miter one end at 45°. With the pointed end on the stool, mark the height of the side casing at the top edge of the head casing.

9

10

11

To get a tight fit for side casings, align one side of a T-bevel with the reveal, mark the side extension and position the other side flush against the horn. Transfer the angle from the T-bevel to the end of the casing, and cut the casing to length.

Test-fit the casings, making any final adjustments with a plane or rasp. Fasten the casing with 4d finish nails at the extensions, and 6d finish nails at the framing members.

Cut the apron to length, leaving a few inches at each end for creating the returns (step 3). Position the apron tight against the bottom edge of the stool, then attach it, using 6d finish nails driven every 12".

12. Installing Arts & Crafts Casing

Traditional Arts & Crafts casings are made of simple, flat materials with little to no decorative molding trimmed out of the stock. Add nonmitered corners to the mix, and this casing becomes as plain as possible. The back band installed on the perimeter of this project is optional, but it adds depth to the window treatment while maintaining simple style.

Traditionally, the wood used for this style of trim is quartersawn oak. The term "quartersawn" refers to the method of milling the material. Quartersawn

oak is easily distinguishable from plain-sawn oak by its tight grain pattern laced with rays of lighter color, also known as rifts. Quarter-sawn oak is more expensive than plain oak, and may only be available at lumberyards or hardwood supply stores, depending upon your area. Either plain sawn or quartersawn oak will fit the style of this casing.

To begin the installation of this trim style, refer to pages 38 and 39 to read the step-by-step process for installing jamb extensions, if necessary, and the stool portion of this project.

Tools & Materials ▸

Tape measure
Straightedge
Power miter saw
Circular saw
    or jigsaw
Hand saw
Plane or rasp
Drill hammer
Pneumatic nailer
Combination square
Compass
Nail set
1 × 4 finish
    lumber

Back band trim
Wood shims
4d, 6d, and 8d
    finish nails
Finishing putty

The Arts & Crafts style is similar to the overall look and feel of Mission furniture, as can be seen in this relatively simple oak window casing.

How to Install Arts & Crafts Casing

1

Follow the step-by-step process on pages 38 to 39 to install the stool and jamb extensions. Set a combination square to ³⁄₁₆" or ¼" and mark a reveal line on the top and side jambs.

2

To find the length of the head casing and apron, measure the distance between the reveal lines on the side jambs and add twice the width of the side casings. Cut the head casing and the apron to length. Install the head casing flush with the top reveal line. Use a scrap piece of trim to line up the head casing horizontally.

3

Measure and cut the side casings to length. Install them flush with the reveal lines. Make sure the joints at the top and bottom are tight. Measure the distance to the end of the stool from the outer edge of the side casing. Install the apron tight to the bottom of the stool at the same dimension from the end of the stool.

4

Back band

Measure, cut, and install the back band around the perimeter of the window casings, mitering the joints at the corners. Continue the back band around the edge of the apron, mitering the corners. Nail the back band in place with 4d finish nails.

13. Installing a Window Shelf

Shelves may be hung above windows as novelty top treatments to showcase plants and collections. They can be used alone or in combination with other window treatments, such as curtains. In that case, mount the shelf with brackets hidden under the valance.

Although the end pieces in this project act as supports for the shelf, also secure the shelf to a horizontal support piece. Then, attach the whole unit to the wall with wood screws. If heavy items are to be displayed, drill more pilot holes for the wood screws to be closer together for added strength.

Whatever the size of the items to be displayed, you can adjust the depth of the shelf unit to accommodate them.

Tools & Materials ▶

Hammer	Nail set
Drill and bits	1 × 8 and
Circular saw	1 × 2 lumber
Jigsaw	2" wood screws
Router	6d casing nails
Sander	Paint or stain

Shelf Variations ▶

Add larger supports at the shelf ends to accommodate a dowel for hanging dried flowers and herbs. A coordinating "backsplash" provides a way to attach the shelf to the wall. Attach hooks to the underside of the shelf to hang other collectibles or keepsakes.

How to Build a Window Shelf

Cut the 1 × 8 shelf board and the 1 × 2 horizontal support piece the same length as the total width of the window unit, including the outer casing. Attach the shelf to the support at a 90° angle, using 2" wood screws spaced every 6" to 10".

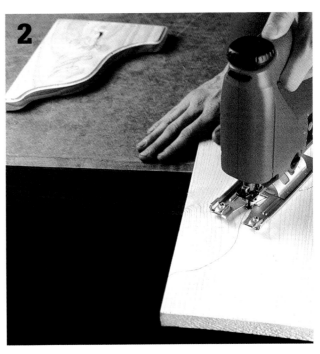

Cut out the two end pieces from 1 × 8 lumber. If the design has only straight lines, use a circular saw. If it includes curves, use a jigsaw.

Add a design to the end supports, using a router. Sand smooth the faces and edges that will be exposed. Attach end supports to shelf unit using wood glue and 6d casing nails. Use a nail set to recess the nail heads. Finish the unit by staining or painting.

Drill pilot holes in the support piece every 6" to 10", avoiding screws attaching the shelf to the horizontal support. Attach shelf unit to wall just above window casing, using 2" wood screws driven through pilot holes. Plug and finish screw holes, if desired.

14. Trimming a Basement Window Opening

Basement windows bring much-needed sunlight into dark areas, but even in finished basements they often get ignored on the trim front. This is partly because most basement foundation walls are at least 8" thick, and often a lot thicker. Add a furred-out wall and the window starts to look more like a tunnel with a pane of glass at the end. But with some well designed and well-executed trim carpentry, you can turn the depth disadvantage into a positive.

A basement window opening may be finished with wallboard, but the easiest way to trim one is by making extrawide custom jambs that extend from the inside face of the window frame to the interior wall surface. Because of the extra width, plywood stock is a good choice for the custom jambs. The project shown here is created with veneer-core plywood with oak veneer surface. The jamb members are fastened together into a nice square frame using rabbet joints at the corner. The frame is scribed and installed as a single unit and then trimmed out with oak casing. The casing is applied flush with the inside edges of the frame opening. If you prefer to have a reveal edge around the interior edge of the casing, you will need to add a solid hardwood strip to the edge of the frame so the plies of the plywood are not visible.

Tools & Materials ▸

Pencil	Finish-grade ¾"
Tape measure	oak plywood
Table saw	Spray-foam insulation
Drill with bits	Composite or cedar
2-ft level	wood shims
Framing square	1¼, 2" finish nails
Utility knife	1⅝" drywall screws
Straightedge	Carpenter's glue

Because they are set into thick foundation walls, basement windows present a bit of a trimming challenge. But the thickness of the foundation wall also lets you create a handy ledge that's deep enough to hold potted plants or even sunning cats.

How to Trim a Basement Window

Check to make sure the window frame and surrounding area are dry and free of rot, mold or damage. At all four corners of the basement window, measure from the inside edges of the window frame to the wall surface. Add 1" to the longest of these measurements.

Set your table saw to make a rip cut to the width arrived at in step 1. If you don't have a table saw, set up a circular saw and straightedge cutting guide to cut strips to this length. With a fine-tooth panel-cutting blade, rip enough plywood strips to make the four jamb frame components.

Miter gauge

Cross-cut the plywood strips to correct lengths. In our case, we designed the jamb frame to be the exact same outside dimensions as the window frame, since there was some space between the jamb frame and the rough opening.

³⁄₈ × ³⁄₄" rabbet

Cut ³⁄₈"-deep × ³⁄₄"-wide rabbets at each end of the head jamb and the sill jamb. A router table is the best tool for this job, but you may use a table saw or hand saws and chisels. Inspect the jambs first and cut the rabbets in whichever face is in better condition. To ensure uniformity, we ganged the two jambs together (they're the same length). It's also a good idea to include backer boards to prevent tear-out.

(continued)

Glue and clamp the frame parts together, making sure to clamp near each end from both directions. Set a carpenter's square inside the frame and check it to make sure it's square.

Before the glue sets, carefully drill three perpendicular pilot holes, countersunk, through the rabbeted workpieces and into the side jambs at each corner. Space the pilot holes evenly, keeping the end ones at least ¾" in from the end. Drive a 1⅝" drywall screw into each pilot hole, taking care not to overdrive. Double check each corner for square as you work, adjusting the clamps if needed.

Let the glue dry for at least one hour (overnight is better), then remove the clamps and set the frame in the window opening. Adjust the frame so it is centered and level in the opening and the exterior-side edges fit flush against the window frame.

Taking care not to disturb the frame's position (rest a heavy tool on the sill to hold it in place if you wish), press a steel rule against the wall surface and mark trimming points at the point where the rule meets the jambs at each side of all four frame corners, using a sharp pencil.

Remove the frame and clamp it on a flat work surface. Use a straightedge to connect the scribe marks at the ends of each jamb frame side. Set the cutting depth of your circular saw to just a small fraction over ¾". Clamp a straightedge guide to the frame so the saw blade will follow the cutting line and trim each frame side in succession. (The advantage to using a circular saw here is that any tear-out from the blade will be on the nonvisible faces of the frame).

Replace the frame in the window opening in the same orientation as when you scribed it and install shims until it is level and centered in the opening. Drive a few finish nails (hand or pneumatic) through the side jambs into the rough frame. Also drive a few nails through the sill jamb. Most trim carpenters do not drive nails into the head jamb.

Insulate between the jamb frame and the rough frame with spray-in polyurethane foam. Look for minimal-expanding foam labeled "window and door" and don't spray in too much. Let the foam dry for a half hour or so and then trim off the excess with a utility knife. *Tip: Protect the wood surfaces near the edges with wide strips of masking tape.*

Remove the masking tape and clean up the mess from the foam (there is always some). Install case molding. We used picture-frame techniques to install fairly simple oak casing.

15. Installing a Decorative Door Header

Adding a decorative head casing to a door is a simple way to dress up your existing trim. Although head treatments are more common over doors, this project will work for window trim as well. Designing your own decorative molding can be creative and fun, but try not to overwhelm the room with an elaborate piece, or it may detract from the décor.

Standard stock door casings have an outer-edge thickness of approximately 1 1/16". Build your custom header around this thickness. Use it to create a reveal line to a thinner piece of trim, or build out from the edge for a bolder, more substantial appear-ance. In the project shown, a bed molding, or smaller piece of crown molding, is used to build out the header away from the wall. The ends of the molding are returned to the wall, and the entire piece is capped with a piece of lattice molding. Installing a decorative header of this style on an interior door may require the installation of additional blocking. For installation over an exterior door or a window, nail the pieces in place directly to the load-bearing framing in the wall above the opening.

Tools & Materials ▸

Pencil	Brad nail gun
Tape measure	Moldings
Power miter saw	Wood glue
Finish nail gun	

Replacing plain head casing on a door or window with a decorative built-up version is a quick and easy way to add some sophistication to any ordinary feature of your home.

How to Install a Decorative Door Header

Measure the width of your door casing and rough-cut a piece of bed or crown molding 6" longer. Use the casing width dimension to layout cut marks on the bottom edge of the molding. Start the marks 2" from the end to allow space for cutting the mitered ends.

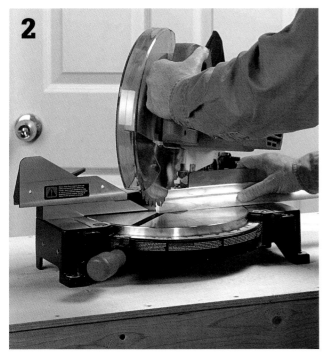

2

With the molding upside down and sprung against the fence, cut a 45° outside corner miter angle at each end, on the casing reference marks from step 1. See pages 20 to 21 for more information on miter-cutting crown molding.

3

Cut mitered returns for the molding using the leftover piece. Set the angle of the power miter saw to the opposing 45° angle and cut the returns with the molding upside down and sprung against the fence. Dry-fit the pieces, recutting them if necessary. Apply glue to the return pieces and nail them to the ends of the head molding with 1" brad nails.

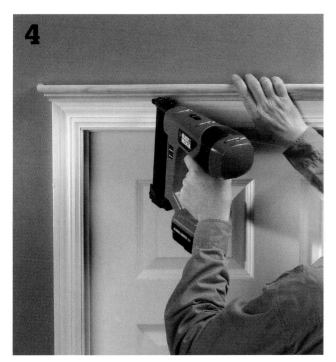

4

Nail the new header in place with 2½" finish nails driven at an angle through the bed molding and into the framing members of the wall.

5

Cut lattice molding 1" longer than the length of the bed molding and nail it in place with ⅝" brad nails so that it has a uniform overhang of ½". Fill all nail holes with spackle and sand them with fine-grit sandpaper. Apply the final coat of finish.

16. Trimming a Wall Opening

Trimming out a wallboard opening is an easy way to add style to any room transition using decorative trim. Although this project may be done with paint-grade materials, clear finish adds detail and inviting wood grain, showcasing the opening.

In the project shown, solid wood trim is used to cover the wallboard jambs of the opening. This technique can also be accomplished with plywood jambs. However, to maintain a constant reveal with the rest of the room, a thin strip of solid oak material should be applied to the edges of the plywood to cover the visible plies. This application should be done prior to installing the jambs to avoid fastening difficulties.

The odds are good that the finished wallboard corners are irregular, causing some minor differences in wall thickness along the jambs of the opening. When these irregularities are minor, (less than $\frac{3}{16}$"), it is best to cut the jamb material at the widest jamb measurement and let the casing bridge the difference. When wall thickness varies a lot ($\frac{3}{16}$" or more), it is better to cut tapered jambs to cover the difference.

Tools & Materials ▸

Pry bar
Side cutters
Pencil
Tape measure
Circular saw and straightedge guide
4-ft. level
Pneumatic finish nail gun
Power miter saw
Framing square
Jamb material (lumber or plywood)
Case moldings
Base moldings
2½" finish nails
Wood glue
Shims
Scrap 2 × 4 material

Before

Passthrough openings between rooms often are left very plain by the builders, especially in more modern homes. Not only is this a dull design statement, it also exposes the edges of the wallboard openings to damage. A little bit of door casing and new jambs can bring new life to the opening (and protect it as well).

How to Trim a Wall Opening

Remove the existing base molding with a pry bar and hammer. Be careful not to mar the surface of the moldings as you remove them. Pull the nails out of the moldings through the back face with an end nippers or side cutters.

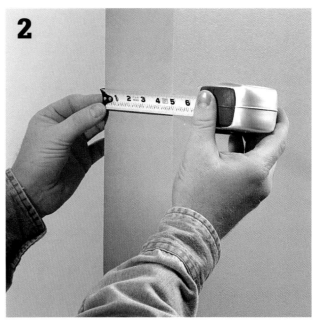

Measure the width and length of the head jamb and the width of each side jamb. Measure each jamb at both ends as well as in the middle of each run. Take note of the measurements. If a jamb differs in width by more than 3/16", install a tapered length (see Tip, below).

Tip ▶

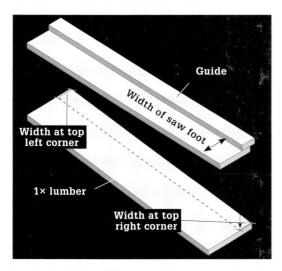

Guide
Width of saw foot
Width at top left corner
1× lumber
Width at top right corner

Jambs that do not taper can be cut on a table saw, but if you have enough variation in your jamb widths that a taper is called for, make a simple cutting jig and taper-cut the jambs to width with a circular saw. Then, lay out the dimensions on the head jamb using the measurements from step 2. The head jamb should run the full length of the opening

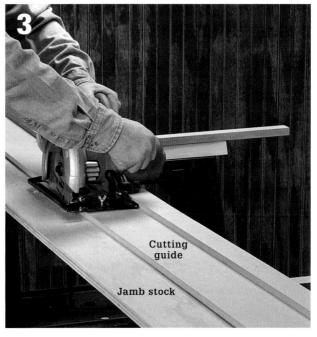

Cutting guide
Jamb stock

Clamp a straightedge guide (Tip, left) to the head jamb on the reference line from the measurements of Step 2, and cut the piece to width with a circular saw. Keep the base plate tight against the fence and move the saw smoothly through the board. Reposition the clamp when you near the end of the board.

(continued)

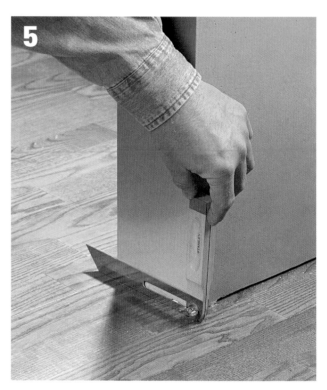

Position the head jamb at the top of the opening, flush with the edges, and nail it in place starting in the middle. Before nailing the ends of the head jamb, check it for square with the walls of the opening, adjusting with shims if necessary. Drive a pair of 2" finish nails every 16".

Place a T-bevel on the floor at the bottom of each side jamb to check for any angled cuts necessary to follow the pitch of the floor. The handle of the bevel should rest against the outer face of the wall, with the blade across the floor.

Transfer the angle from the T-bevel in step 5 to a power miter saw and cut the side jambs to length. The top end of the jamb should be cut square (90°). Each jamb should butt against the head jamb and fit tightly to the finished flooring.

7

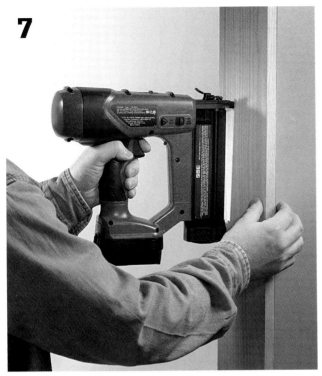

Nail the side jambs in place using pairs of 2" finish nails driven every 16" along the jamb. Check the edges of the jamb pieces as you go to make sure they are flush with the surface of the wall.

8

Install casing around the opening. Maintain a consistent ³⁄₁₆" to ¼" reveal around the opening.

9

Measure, cut, and reinstall the existing baseboard so that the ends butt into the sides of the casing. Cut and reinstall the base shoe using mitered or beveled returns.

10

Fill all nail holes with finishing putty and apply a final coat of polyurethane or your finish of choice (try to match existing trim in the room).

17. Hanging Interior Prehung Doors

Prehung doors come as single units with the door already hung on hinges attached to a factory-built frame. To secure the unit during shipping, most prehung doors are braced or nailed shut with a couple of duplex nails driven through the jambs and into the door edge. These nails must be removed before you install the door.

The key to installing doors is to plumb and fasten the hinge-side jamb first. After that's in place, you can position the top and latch-side jambs by checking the reveal—the gap between the closed door and the jamb.

Standard prehung doors have 4½"-wide jambs and are sized to fit walls with 2 × 4 construction and ½" wallboard. If you have thicker walls, you can special-order doors to match, or you can add jamb extensions to standard-size doors.

Tools & Materials ▸

4-ft. level
Nail set
Handsaw
Prehung door unit

Wood shims
8d and 10d
   casing nails

Solid-core interior doors are heavier than hollow-core doors and may cause the jamb to bow, throwing the unit out of alignment. To fix this problem, loosely nail the top and bottom of the hinge-side jamb in place. Use a pry bar on the bottom of the door to lift the weight off the jamb. While the weight is lifted, drive two 10d casing nails near the top hinge. This will relieve the weight of the door and you may continue installation as with a hollow-core unit.

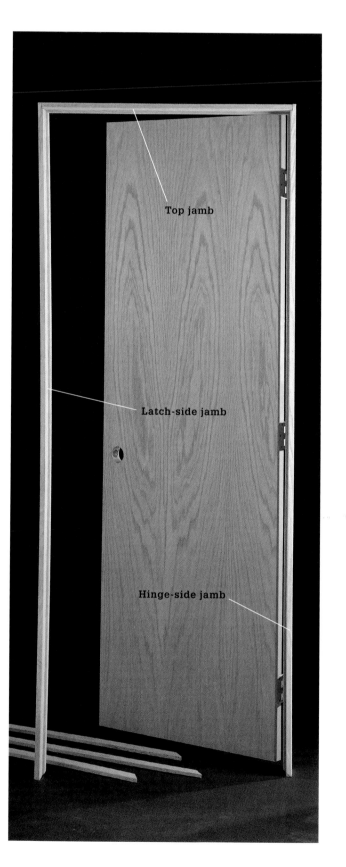

Top jamb

Latch-side jamb

Hinge-side jamb

How to Install a Prehung Interior Door

1

Set the door unit into the framed opening so the jamb edges are flush with the wall surfaces and the unit is centered from side to side. Using a level, adjust the unit so the hinge-side jamb is plumb.

2

Starting near the top hinge, insert pairs of shims driven from opposite directions into the gap between the framing and jamb, sliding shims in until they are snug. Check the jamb to make sure it remains plumb and does not bow inward. Install shims near each hinge and the top and bottom of the jamb.

3

Anchor the hinge-side jamb with 8d casing nails driven through the jamb and shims and into the framing. Drive nails only at the shim locations.

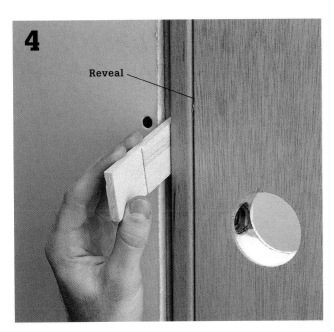

4

Reveal

Insert pairs of shims into the gap between the framing members and the top jamb and latch-side jamb, aligning them roughly with the hinge-side shims. With the door closed, adjust the shims so the reveal is consistent. Drive casing nails through the jambs and shims and into the framing members.

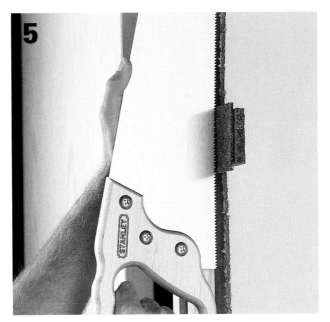

5

Set all nails below the surface of the wood with a nail set, then cut off the shims flush with the wall surface, using a handsaw or utility knife. Hold the saw vertically to prevent damage to the door jamb or wall. See page 34 to install the door casing.

18. Installing Plastic & Miterless Molding

Although traditional moldings are made from solid wood, your options (especially for paint-grade projects) do not end there. There is a wide variety of plastic molding available as well as molding made from wood products such as medium density fiberboard, or MDF. These alternative moldings are sold at home centers near the solid wood products.

One of the biggest advantages of alternative materials for trim moldings is cost. Intricate detailed moldings are considerably less expensive than their wood counterparts. Larger, more elaborate trim that is not available in solid wood (because it would be too expensive), is available in an assortment of styles right off the shelf, or custom ordered. Ceiling medallions and decorative corbels are examples of other plastic products that would otherwise not be commonly available. Ready-to-assemble mantels and decorative door caps are also offered. These products add style to any room immediately and are simple to install.

Another advantage of some plastic material and MDF is dimensional stability. With the change of humidity and temperature in the seasons, solid wood products expand and contract at varying rates. This causes joints to open up over time and, in some cases, split around a fastener. Some alternative materials are known to expand and contract less than wood. These materials are more dimensionally stable, which means that your project will most likely look better with tighter joints for a longer period of time.

For the most part, solid wood alternatives can be cut, machined, and installed just as solid wood products are. Many plastics will not split when fastened like wood, making installation easier. Some products may melt when cut slowly with a power saw, so it's a good idea to make cuts with moderate speed at a uniform rate.

Be cautious when purchasing plastic trim. Each material has pros and cons that you should be aware of. For example, some plastics such as polystyrene are less expensive but less durable than solid wood. They are also available with a prefinished wood grain appearance, unlike most other plastic products. Consult a home center specialist to help you choose the best material for your particular application.

Miterless moldings are another option that is commonly available with alternative materials. Miterless moldings utilize corner "blocks" and transition moldings to eliminate the need for complex cuts at corners or between pieces of molding. Plastic blocks may be used along with plastic molding or in combination with solid wood. After the project is painted, the difference in materials will be unnoticeable. Miterless moldings are available in solid wood as well. Plinth blocks and corner posts are available for base trim installation. Door and window casings can be trimmed out with rosette corners or decorative head treatments that cap the legs of the casing.

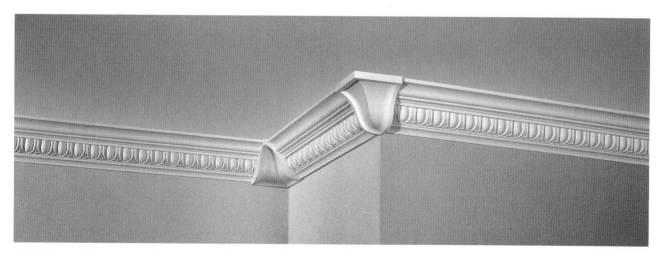

Miterless moldings are gaining in popularity because they are so simple to install. Instead of making tricky miter cuts or cope cuts, you simply butt each piece of trim to a corner block or transition block.

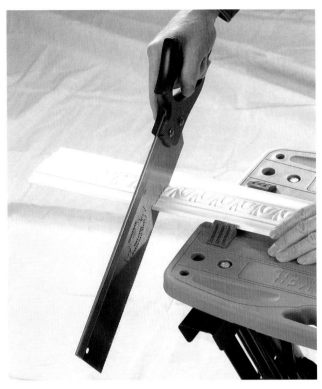

Plastic moldings can be cut, machined, and nailed just like wood moldings. Unlike wood moldings, plastics won't split when nailed near an edge.

Prefabricated MDF moldings are very dimensionally stable compared to solid wood products and sand easily. For best results, prime and paint the molding prior to installation.

Ornamental corbels don't have any practical value, but they provide strong visual appeal and can also be used to create small decorative shelves.

Rosettes made from wood products or urethane can be installed at the corners of window and door openings to eliminate the need for precise miter angles.

19. Hanging French Doors

Traditionally, French doors open onto the patio or lush garden of a backyard. But you can create stylish entrances inside your home by bringing French doors to formal dining rooms, sitting rooms or dens, and master suites.

French doors are made up of two separate doors, hinged on opposing jambs of a doorway. The doors swing out from the center of the doorway and into or out from a room. Like most doors, French doors are typically sold in prehung units, but are also available separately. They are generally available only in wood, with a variety of designs and styles to choose from.

Before purchasing a prehung French door unit, determine the size of doors you will need. If you are planning to install the doors in an existing doorway, measure the dimensions of the rough opening, from the unfinished framing members, then order the unit to size—the manufacturer or distributor will help you select the proper unit.

You can also pick the prehung unit first, then alter an existing opening to accommodate it (as shown in this project). In this case, build the rough opening a little larger than the actual dimensions of the doors to accommodate the jambs. Prehung units typically require adding 1" to the width and ½" to the height.

If the doorway will be in a load-bearing wall, you will need to make temporary supports, and install an appropriately sized header. Sizing the header (depth) is critical: it's based on the length of the header, the material it's made from, and the weight of the load it must support. For actual requirements, consult your local building department.

When installing French doors, it is important to have consistent reveals between the two doors and between the top of the doors and the head jamb. This allows the doors to close properly and prevents the hinges from binding.

Tools & Materials ▸

Tape measure
Circular saw
4-ft. level
Hammer
Handsaw
Drill
Utility knife
Nail set
½" plywood
Prehung French door unit
2 × 4 and
    2 × 6 lumber
10d & 16d common nails
Wood shims
8d finish nails

How to Frame & Install French Doors

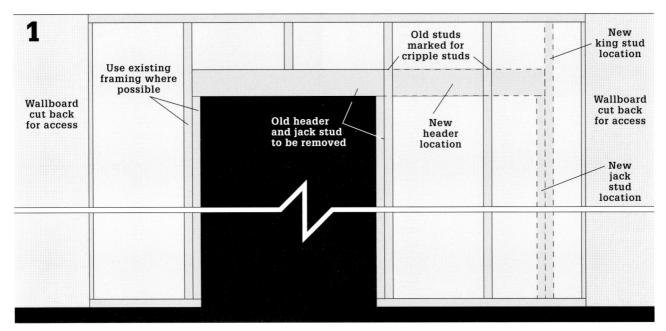

1

Wallboard cut back for access

Use existing framing where possible

Old header and jack stud to be removed

Old studs marked for cripple studs

New header location

New king stud location

Wallboard cut back for access

New jack stud location

Shut off power and water to the area. Remove the wall surfaces from both sides of the wall, leaving one stud bay open on each side of the new rough opening. Also remove or reroute any wiring, plumbing, or ductwork. Lay out the new rough opening, marking the locations of all new jack and king studs on both the top and bottom plates. Where practical, use existing framing members. To install a new king stud, cut a stud to size and align with the layout marks, toenail to the bottom plate with 10d common nails, check for plumb, then toenail to the top plate to secure. Finally, mark both the bottom and top of the new header on one king stud, then use a level to extend the lines across the intermediate studs to the opposite king stud. If using existing framing, measure and mark from the existing jack stud.

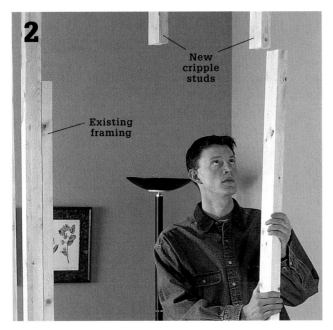

2

New cripple studs

Existing framing

Cut the intermediate studs at the reference marks for the top of the header, using a reciprocating saw. Pry the studs away from the sole plates and remove—the remaining top pieces will be used as cripple studs.

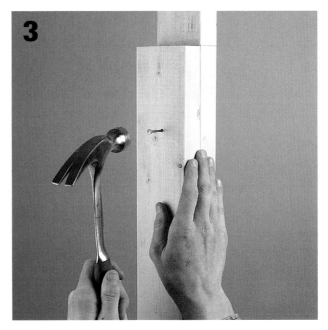

3

To install a jack stud, cut the stud to fit between the sole plate and the bottom of the header, as marked on the king stud. Align it at the mark against the king stud, then fasten it in place with 10d common nails driven every 12".

(continued)

4

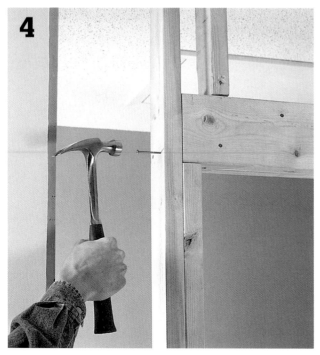

Build the header to size and install, fastening it to the jack studs, king studs, and cripple studs, using 16d common nails. Use a handsaw to cut through the bottom plate so it's flush with the inside faces of the jack studs. Remove the cutout portion.

5

Finish the walls before installing the doors, then set the prehung door unit into the framed opening so the jamb edges are flush with the finished wall surfaces and the unit is centered from side to side.

6

Using a level, adjust the unit to plumb one of the side jambs. Starting near the top of the door, insert pairs of shims driven from opposite directions into the gap between the framing and the jamb, sliding the shims until they are snug. Check the jamb to make sure it remains plumb and does not bow inward.

7

Working down along the jamb, install shims near each hinge and near the floor. Make sure the jamb is plumb, then anchor it with 8d finish nails driven through the jamb and shims and into the framing. Leave the nail heads partially protruding so the jamb can be readjusted later if necessary.

8

Install shims at the other side jamb, aligning them roughly with the shims of the first jamb. With the doors closed, adjust the shims so the reveal between the doors is even and the tops of the doors are aligned.

9

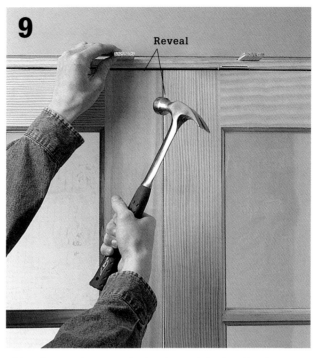

Shim the gap between the header and the head jamb to create a consistent reveal along the top when the doors are closed. Insert pairs of shims every 12". Drive 8d finish nails through the jambs and shims and into the framing members.

10

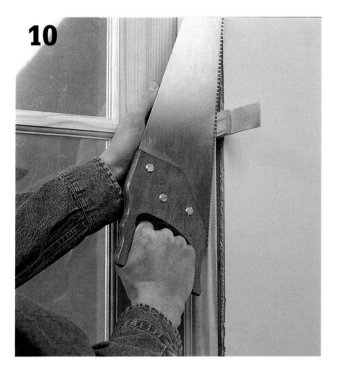

Drive all the nails fully, then set them below the surface of the wood with a nail set. Cut off the shims flush with the wall surface, using a handsaw or utility knife. Hold the saw vertically to prevent damage to the door jamb or wall. Install the door casing.

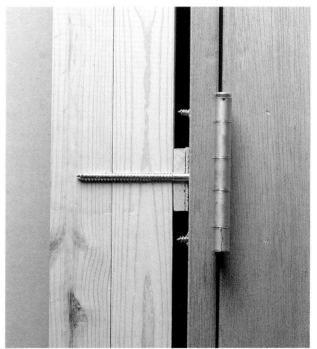

Option: Replace the center mounting screw on each hinge with a 3" wood screw to provide extra support for door hinges and jambs. These long screws extend through the side jambs and deep into the framing members. Be careful not to overtighten screws—overtightening will cause the jambs to bow.

20. Installing Wainscoting with Tongue & Groove Boards

A wainscot, by definition, is a wall treatment covering the lower portion of a wall. Virtually any material can be used as wainscoting, but the most common by far is wood. In most applications, the wainscot is covered along the bottom by a baseboard and along the top by a cap molding, rail, or shallow shelf.

Wainscots are useful not only for decoration but also as protective surfaces. Standard wainscot heights are between 32" and 36", a range at which the top cap can serve as a chair rail to protect the wall from furniture collisions. In hallways, mudrooms, and other functional areas, wainscots may run 48" and higher.

Wood wainscoting is available in a variety of species and styles. For price and ease of installation, the best types for do-it-yourselfers are 4 × 8-ft. sheets and tongue-and-groove boards, commonly called beadboard. Standard materials include paint-grade pine (and other softwoods); hardwood veneers, such as oak and birch; molded polymers; and fiberboard.

There are two basic methods for installing wainscoting. Sheets and thinner boards (up to ⅜", in most cases) can be attached to drywall with construction adhesive and nails, or with nails alone. Thicker boards usually must be nailed, preferably blind-nailed—the technique of driving angled nails along the base of the tongue so the groove of the next board hides the nail heads. Thinner boards may have to be facenailed to avoid splitting the wood.

Wainscoting that is fastened only with nails must have blocking or backing to serve as a nailing surface. If the framing is exposed, you can install plywood backing over the wall studs in the area of the wainscot, then cover the rest of the wall with drywall of the same thickness (make sure the local building code permits installing wood directly over wall framing). You can also install 2 × 4 blocks between the studs, at 12" to 16" intervals, before hanging the drywall.

The project on pages 65 to 67 shows you specific methods for installing tongue-and-groove beadboard, such as dealing with electrical outlets and trimming around windows. Pages 68 and 69 deal with installing sheet paneling with traditional moldings applied to the top and bottom edges. Because of its height, and tall baseboard, this wainscot is especially suited to mudroom or hallway walls that receive some abuse, but it can work well in bathrooms as well. Install hooks for coats or towels along the rail or add a shelf for additional storage.

Tongue-and-groove wainscoting boards are milled with smooth faces, or contoured to add additional texture to your walls. For staining, choose a wood species with a pronounced grain. For painting, poplar is a good choice, since it has few knots and a highly consistent grain.

Tools & Materials ▸

Pencil	Tongue-and-groove
Chalk line	boards
Level	Sheet paneling
Miter saw or miter box	Construction
Jigsaw	adhesive
Circular saw	10d, 6d, 4d, and 2d
Caulk gun	finish nails
Drill	1 × 6 and 1 × 3 clear
Router with	pine lumber
roundover bit	Wood glue
Hammer	Cove molding
Nail set	Baseboard
Compass	Receptacle box
Plane	extenders
Circuit tester	(as required)
Pry bar	Baseboard and cap
Tape measure	rail molding
Paint brush	Paint or stain

How to Prepare for a Wainscoting Project

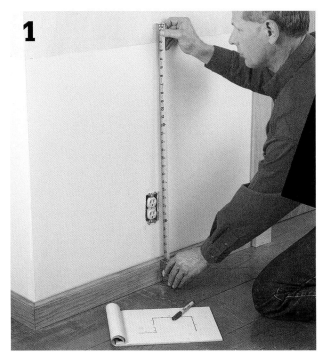

1

Measure to make a plan drawing of each wall in your project. Indicate the locations of fixtures, receptacles, and windows. Use a level to make sure the corners are plumb. If not, mark plumb lines on the walls to use as reference points.

2

Condition the planking by stacking it in the room where it will be installed. Place spacers between the planks to let air circulate around each board, allowing the wood to adjust to the room's temperature and humidity. Wait 72 hours before staining or sealing the front, back, and edges of each plank.

3

Remove the baseboard moldings, along with any receptacle cover plates, vent covers, or other wall fixtures within the area you plan to cover. Before you begin, turn off the electricity to the circuits in the area.

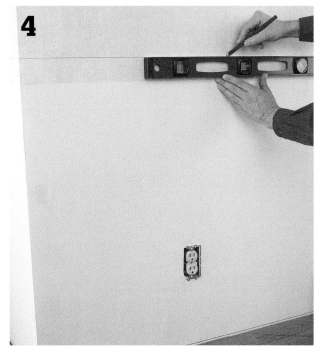

4

Mark the walls with level lines to indicate the top of the wainscoting. Mark a line ¼" from the floor to provide a small gap for expansion at the floor.

(continued)

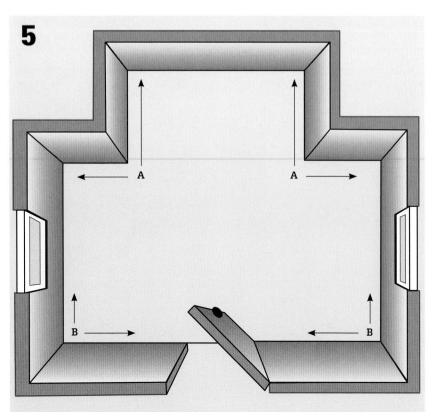

5

Begin installation at the corners.
Install any outside corners (A) first, working your way toward the inside corners. In sections of a room that have no outside corners, start at the inside corners (B), and work your way toward the door and window casings. Calculate the number of boards required for each wall, using the measurements on the drawing you created earlier (length of wall ÷ width of one plank). When making this calculation, remember that the tongues are removed from the corner boards. If the total number of boards for a wall includes a fraction of less than ½ of a board, plan to trim the first and last boards to avoid ending with a board cut to less than half its original width.

How to Install Wainscoting at Outside Corners

Cut a pair of boards to the widths indicated in the calculations you developed during the planning process.

Position the boards at the corner, butting them to create a plumb corner. Facenail the boards in place, then nail the joint, using 6d finish nails. Drive the nails to within ⅛" of the face of the boards, then finish with a nail set.

Position a piece of corner trim and nail it in place, using 6d finish nails. Install the remaining boards (opposite, steps 5 and 6).

How to Install Wainscoting at Inside Corners

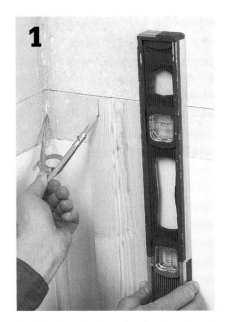

1

Hold a level against the first board and hold the board flush with the corner. If the wall is out of plumb, trim the board to compensate: hold the board plumb, position a compass at the inside corner of the wall, and use it to scribe a line down the board.

2

Cut along the scribed line with a circular saw.

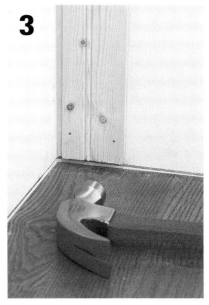

3

Hold the first board in the corner, leaving a ¼" gap for expansion, and facenail into the center of the board at each nailer location, using 6d finish nails. Drive the top nails roughly ½" from the edge so they'll be hidden from view once the cap rail is attached.

4

Install a second board at the corner by butting it against the first one, then facenailing in at least two locations. Nail to within ⅛" of the face of the board, then use a nail set to finish.

5

Position subsequent boards. Leave a ¹⁄₁₆" gap at each joint to allow for seasonal expansion. Use a level to check every third board for plumb. If the wainscoting is out of plumb, adjust the fourth board, as necessary, to compensate.

6

Mark and cut the final board to fit. If you're at a door casing, cut the board to fit flush with the casing (trim off at least the tongue). If you're at an inside corner, make sure it is plumb. If not, scribe and trim the board to fit.

How to Make a Cutout

Test the receptacle (inset) to make sure the power is off. Then, unscrew and remove the receptacle from the box. Coat the edges of the electrical box with bright-colored chalk.

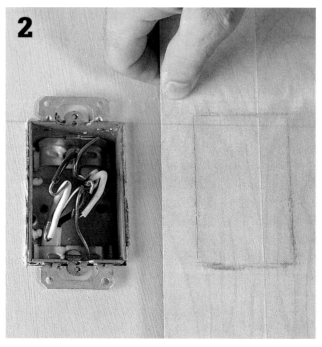

Press the back of the board that will be installed over the receptacle directly against the electrical box, to create a cutting outline.

Lay the board face-down and drill a large pilot hole near one corner of the outline. Use a jigsaw fitted with a fine-tooth woodcutting blade to make the cutout. Be careful not to cut outside the lines.

Facenail the wainscoting to the wall, then reattach the receptacle with the tabs overlapping the wainscoting so the receptacle is flush with the opening. You may need longer screws.

Tip ▶

When paneling around a receptacle with thick stock, you will need to attach a receptacle box extender to the inside of the box, then reconnect the receptacle so it is flush with the opening in the paneling.

How to Install Wainscoting Around a Window

On casement windows, install wainscoting up to the casings on the sides and below the window. Install ½" cove molding or other trim to finish the edges.

On double-hung windows, install wainscoting up to the side casings. You can notch the wainscoting to fit around the stool, or remove the stool and notch it to fit over the wainscoting. Remove the apron (below the stool) and reinstall it over the wainscoting.

How to Finish a Wainscoting Project

1

Cut baseboard moldings to fit over the wainscoting and attach them by nailing 6d finishing nails at the stud locations. If you plan to install base shoe, leave a small gap at the floor.

2

Cut the cap rail to fit as you would contoured baseboard. At doors and windows, install the cap rail so its edge is flush with the side casings.

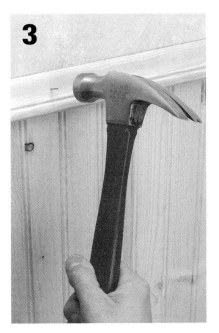

3

Attach the cap rail by nailing 4d finish nails through the flats of the moldings at the stud locations. Set the nails with a nail set.

How to Install a Wainscot with Sheet Paneling

1

Measure up from the floor and snap a chalk line to represent the top of the paneling. This line will be ¾" lower than the overall height of the wainscot. Use a pencil to mark the stud locations about 1" above the chalk line. Measure the length of the wall to plan the layout of the sheets. The last piece should be at least 3" wide, so you may have to trim the first sheet to make the last piece wider.

2

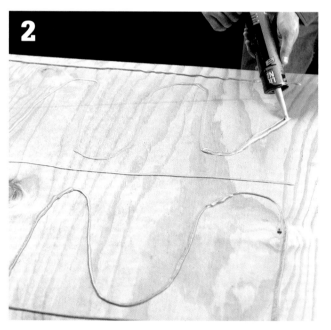

Check the wall corner with a level to make sure it's plumb. If it's not plumb, scribe the first sheet to follow the angle or contours of the wall. Cut the first sheet to length so its bottom edge will be ½" above the floor, using a circular saw. Unless you've scribed the sheet, cut from the back side to prevent splintering on the face. Using a caulk gun, apply construction adhesive to the back side.

3

Apply the sheet to the wall so its top edge is flush with the chalk line and its side edge is set into the corner. Press the sheet firmly to bond it to the wall. Drive 6d finish nails at the stud locations, spacing them every 16" or so. Use only as many nails as needed to hold the sheet flat and to keep it in place.

4

Install the remaining sheets in the wall section. If you are paneling an adjacent wall, check the paneled wall for plumb, and trim the first sheet, if necessary. Install the sheet butted against the end sheet on the paneled wall.

5

Prepare the 1 × 6 rail material by sanding smooth the front face and bottom edge. If desired, round over the bottom, outside corner slightly with sandpaper. Install the rail with its top edge flush with the chalk line, fastening it to each stud with two 10d finish nails driven through pilot holes. Butt together rail pieces at inside corners, and miter them at outside corners, following the same techniques used for cutting and fitting baseboard (see "Installing Base Molding," page 6).

6

Mill the 1 × 3 top cap material, using a router and roundover bit. Work on test pieces to find the desired amount of roundover, then rout your workpieces on both front corners. Sand the cap smooth. *Option: Create a waterfall edge by rounding over only the top edge of the cap (top inset), or chamfer the front edges with a chamfer bit (bottom inset).*

7

Install the cap with wood glue and finish nails. Glue along the top edge of the rail and drive a 10d finish nail, angled at 45°, through the cap and into each stud (drill pilot holes for the nails). Miter the rail at corners.

8

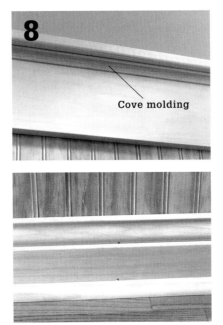

Cove molding

Add cove molding to the joint between the cap and rail, fastening it to the rail with 2d finish nails. Install the baseboard along the bottom of the wainscot. Set all nails with a nail set.

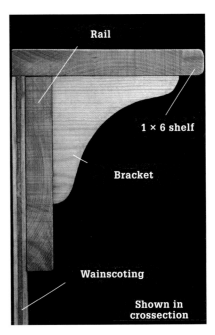

Rail

1 × 6 shelf

Bracket

Wainscoting

Shown in crossection

Variation: Top your wainscot with a shelf rather than a cap. Use 1 × 6 or wider boards, and mill them as shown in step 6. To support the shelf, add wooden brackets fastened to the wall studs.

21. Installing Wall Frame Moldings

Adding wall frame moldings is a traditional decorative technique used to highlight special features of a room, divide large walls into smaller sections, or simply to add interest to plain surfaces. You can paint the molding the same color as the walls or use a contrasting color. For even greater contrast, paint or wallcover the areas within the frames.

Decorative wood moldings with curved contours work best for wall frames. Chair rail, picture rail, base shoe, cove, quarter-round, and other suitable molding types are readily available at home centers and lumberyards in several wood species.

To determine the sizes and locations of the frames, cut strips of paper to the width of the molding and tape them to the wall. You may want the frames to match the dimensions of architectural details in the room, such as windows or a fireplace.

Install the molding with small finish nails driven at each wall stud location and at the ends of the pieces. Use nails long enough to penetrate the studs by ¾". If there aren't studs where you need them, secure the molding with dabs of construction adhesive.

Tools & Materials ▸

Level
Framing square
Miter box and backsaw
Drill and bits
Nail set
Paper strips
Tape
Wood finishing materials
Construction adhesive
Paintable latex caulk or wood putty

How to Install Wall Frame Moldings

Cut paper strips to the width of the molding, and tape them to the wall. Use a framing square and level to make sure the frame is level and the strips are square to one another. Mark the outer corners of the frame with light pencil lines.

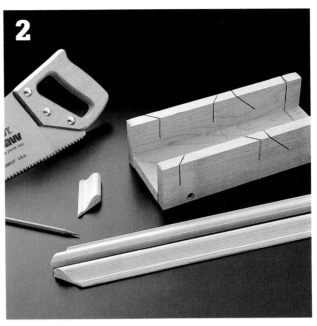

Cut the molding pieces to length, using a miter box and a backsaw (or power miter saw) to cut the ends at 45°. The top and bottom pieces should be the same length, as should the side pieces. Test fit the pieces, and make any necessary adjustments.

Paint or stain the moldings as desired. Position the top molding piece on the placement marks and tack it in place with two finish nails. If necessary, drill pilot holes for the nails to prevent splitting.

Tack the side moldings in place, using the framing square to make sure they are square to the top piece. Tack up the bottom piece. Adjust the frame, if necessary, so that all of the joints fit tightly, then completely fasten the pieces.

Drive the nails slightly below the surface, using a nail set. Fill the nail holes (and corner joints, if necessary) with wood putty. Touch up the patched areas with paint or stain.

22. Installing Wainscot Frames

Frame-and-panel wainscot adds depth, character, and a sense of Old-World charm to any room. Classic wainscot was built with grooved or rabbeted rails and stiles that captured a floating hardwood panel. In the project shown here, the classic appearance is mimicked, but the difficulties of machining precise parts and commanding craftsman-level joinery are eliminated. Paint-grade materials (mostly MDF) are used in the project shown; however you can also build the project with solid hardwoods and finish-grade plywood if you prefer a clear-coat finish.

Installing wainscot frames that look like frame-and-panel wainscot can be done piece by piece, but it is often easier to assemble the main frame parts in your shop. Not only does working in the shop allow you to join the frame parts together (we use pocket screws driven in the backs of the rails and stiles), it generally results in a more professional look.

Once the main frames are assembled, they can be attached to the wall at stud locations. If you prefer to site-build the wainscot piece by piece, you may need to replace the wallcovering material with plywood to create nailing surfaces for the individual pieces.

We primed all of the wainscot parts prior to installing them and then painted the wainscot (including the wall sections within the wainscot panel frames) a contrasting color from the wall above the wainscot cap.

Tools & Materials ▸

Laser level
Pencil
Tape measure
Circular saw
    or table saw
Straightedge guide
Power miter saw
Drill with bits
Carpenter's square
Pocket hole jig
    with screws
Pry bar
Hammer

Pneumatic finish
    nail gun with
    compressor
Caulking gun
¾"-thick MDF
    sheet stock
1¹⁄₁₆" cove molding
½ × ¾" base shoe
⁹⁄₁₆ × 1⅛" cap molding
    (10 ft. per panel)
Panel adhesive
Paint and primer

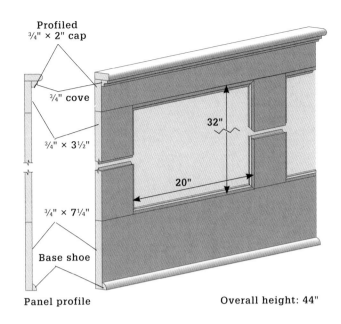

Profiled
¾" × 2" cap

¾" cove

¾" × 3½"

¾" × 7¼"

Base shoe

Panel profile

32"

20"

Overall height: 44"

How to Install Wainscot Frames

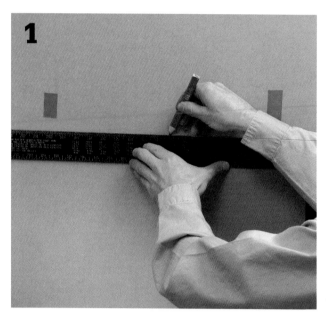

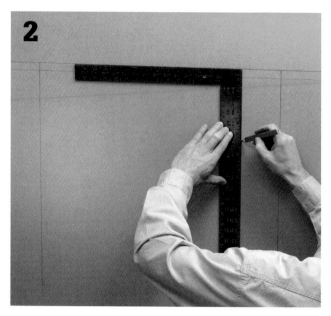

Use a laser level and a pencil to mark the height of the wainscot installation directly onto all walls in the project area. Also mark the height of the top rail (¾" below the overall height), since the cap rail will be installed after the rest of the wainscot is installed. Mark stud locations, using an electronic stud finder.

Plot out the wainscot layout on paper and then test the layout by drawing lines on the wall to make sure you're happy with the design. Try to use a panel width that can be divided evenly into all project wall lengths. In some cases, you may need to make the panel widths slightly different from wall to wall, but make sure to maintain a consistent width within each wall's run.

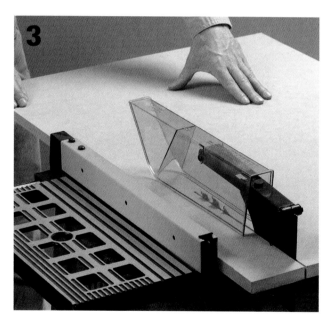

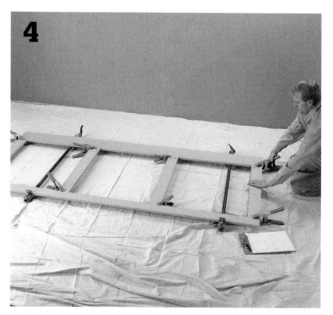

Based on your plan, rip a sheet of MDF into strips to make all of the wainscot parts except the trim moldings. In our case, that included the cap rail (2" wide), the top rail and stiles (3½" wide), and the base rail (7¼" wide). *Note: These are standard lumber dimensions. You can use 1 × 4 and 1 × 4 dimensional lumber for the rails and stiles (use 1 × 2 or rip stock for the cap rail).*

Cut top rails, base rails, and stiles (but not cap rails) to length and dry-assemble the parts into ladder frames based on your layout. Plan the layouts so wall sections longer than 8 ft. are cut with scarf joints in the rails meeting at a stud location. Dry-assemble the pieces on a flat work surface.

5

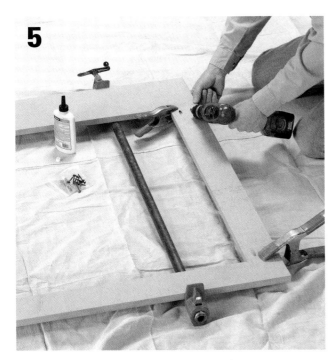

Assemble the frames using glue and pocket screws or biscuits. Clamp the parts together first and check with a carpenter's square to make sure the stiles are perpendicular to both rails.

6

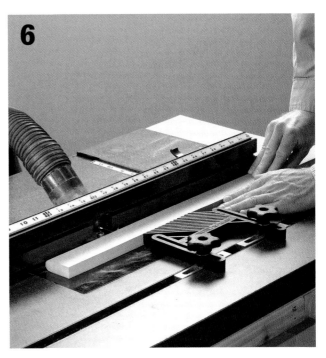

Mount a ¾" roundover bit in your router or router table and shape a bullnose profile on the front edge of your cap rail stock.

7

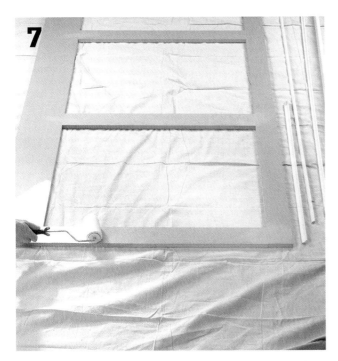

Prime all parts on both sides, including the milled moldings and uncut cap rail stock.

8

Position the frames against the wall and shim underneath the bottom rails as necessary to bring them flush with the top rail marks on the wall (¾" below the overall height lines). Attach the wainscot sections by driving 3" drywall screws, countersunk, through the top rail and the bottom rail at each stud location. If you are using scarf joints, be sure to install the open half first.

(continued)

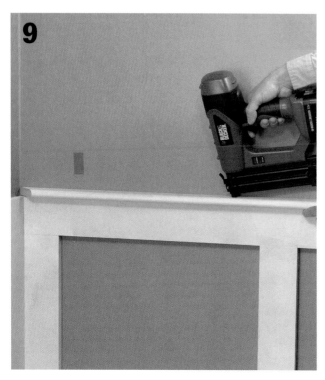

Cut the cap rail to length and attach it to the top rail with panel adhesive and finish nails. Drive a 3" drywall screw through the cap rail and into the wall toenails style at each location. Be sure to carefully drill pilot holes and countersink holes for each screw. Miter-cut the cap rails at the corners.

Install cove molding in the crotch where the cap rail and top rails meet, using glue and a brad nailer. Then, nail base shoe to conceal any gaps between the bottoms, trials and the floor. Miter all corners.

Cut mitered frames to fit around the perimeter of each panel frame created by the rails and stiles. Use cap molding.

Mask the wall above the cap rail and then prime and paint the wainscot frames. Generally, a lighter, contrasting color than the wall color above is most effective visually.

Variation: Natural Wood Finish

Snap a level line at the top rail height. Because the rails and stiles are the same thickness, the backer panel should run all the way from the floor to just shy of the top of the top rail. Cut the backers so the grain will run vertically when installed. Attach them to the walls with panel adhesive, notching to fit around obstructions such as this window opening.

Install the baseboard and top rail directly over the backer panels, using a finish nailer or by hand-nailing with 6d finish nails. The top edge of the top rail pieces should be slightly higher then the backer panels. Use your reference line as a guide for the top rail, but double-check with a level.

Attach the cap rail pieces with a finish nailer. The caps should butt flush against the wall, concealing the top edges of the backer panels. Also butt the cap rails against the window and door casings.

Cut the stile to fit between the top rail and the baseboard and install them. It's okay to vary the spacing slightly form wall to wall, but try to keep them evenly spaced on each wall. Where the wainscot meets door or window casing, butt the edges of the stiles against the casing. This can mean notching around window aprons or horns as well as door plinth blocks.

Add decorative touches, such as the corbels we cut for this installation. The corbels provide some support for the cap rail but their function is primarily decorative. We glued and nailed one corbel at each end of each cap rail piece and above each stile, and then added an intermediate one between each pair of stiles.

23. Paneling a Ceiling

Tongue-and-groove paneling offers a warm, attractive finish that's especially suited to vaulted ceilings. Pine is the most common material for tongue-and-groove paneling, but you can choose from many different wood species and panel styles. Panels typically are ⅜" to ¾" thick and are often attached directly to ceiling joists or rafters. Some building codes require the installation of drywall as a fire stop behind ceiling paneling that's thinner than ¼".

When purchasing your paneling, get enough material to cover about 15% more square footage than the actual ceiling size, to allow for waste. Since the tongue portions of the panels slip into the grooves of adjacent pieces, square footage for paneling is based on the reveal—the exposed face of the panel after it is installed.

Tongue-and-groove boards can be attached with flooring nails or finish nails. Flooring nails hold better because they have spiraled shanks, but they tend to have larger heads than finish nails. Whenever possible, drive the nails through the base of the tongue and into the framing. This is called blind-nailing, because the groove of the succeeding board covers the nail heads. Add facenails only at joints and in locations where more support is needed, such as along the first and last boards. To ensure clean cuts, use a compound miter saw. These saws are especially useful for ceilings with non-90° angles.

Layout is crucial to the success of a paneling project. Before you start, determine how many boards you'll need, using the reveal measurement. If the final board will be less than 2" wide, trim the first, or starter, board by cutting the long edge that abuts the wall. If the ceiling peak is not parallel to the side (starting) wall, rip the starter piece at an angle to match the wall. The leading edge of the starter piece, and every piece thereafter, must be parallel to the peak.

Tools & Materials ▸

Chalk line
Compound
  miter saw,
Circular saw
Drill
Nail set

Pneumatic finish nail
  gun (optional)
Tongue-and-groove
  paneling
1¾" spiral flooring nails
Trim molding

How to Panel a Ceiling

1

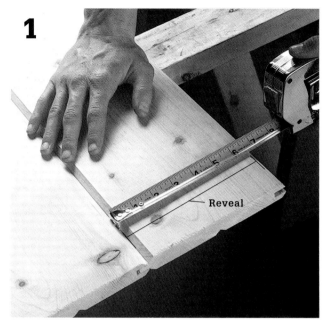

To plan your layout, first measure the reveal of the boards. Fit two pieces together and measure from the bottom edge of the upper board to the bottom edge of the lower board. Calculate the number of boards needed to cover one side of the ceiling by dividing the reveal dimension into the overall distance between the top of the wall and the peak.

2

Use the calculation from step 1 to make a control line for the first row of panels—the starter boards. At both ends of the ceiling, measure down from the peak an equal distance, and make a mark to represent the top (tongue) edges of the starter boards. Snap a chalk line through the marks.

3

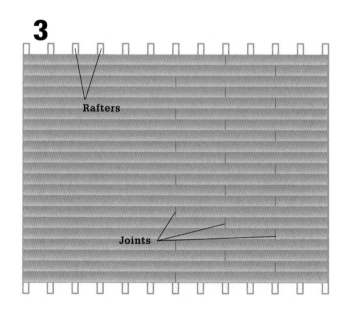

If the boards aren't long enough to span the entire ceiling, plan the locations of the joints. Staggering the joints in a three-step pattern will make them less conspicuous. Note that each joint must fall over the middle of a rafter. For best appearance, select boards of similar coloring and grain for each row.

4

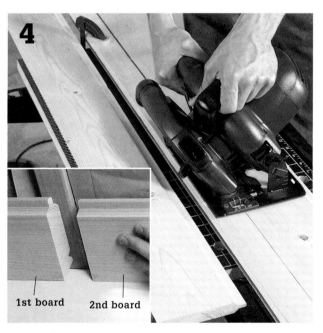

Rip the first starter board to width by bevel-cutting the bottom (grooved) edge. If the starter row will have joints, cut the board to length using a 30° bevel cut on the joint end only. Two beveled ends joined together form a scarf joint (inset), which is less noticeable than a butt joint. If the board spans the ceiling, square-cut both ends.

(continued)

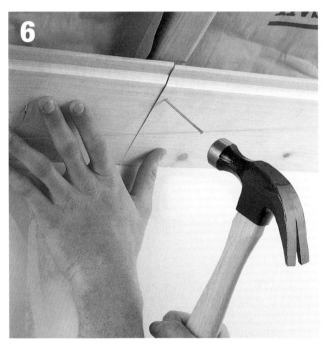

Position the first starter board so the tongue is on the control line. Leave a ⅛" gap between the square board end and the end wall. Fasten the board by nailing through its face about 1" from the grooved edge and into the rafters. Then, blind-nail through the base of the tongue into each rafter, angling the nail backward at 45°. Drive the nail heads beneath the wood surface, using a nail set.

Cut and install any remaining boards in the starter row one at a time, making sure the scarf joints fit together tightly. At each scarf joint, drive two nails through the face of the top board, angling the nail to capture the end of the board behind it. If necessary, predrill the nail holes to prevent splitting.

Cut the first board for the next row, then fit its grooved edge over the tongue of the board in the starter row. Use a hammer and a scrap piece of paneling to drive downward on the tongue edge, seating the grooved edge over the tongue of the starter board. Fasten the second row with blind-nails only.

As you install successive rows, measure down from the peak to make sure the rows remain parallel to the peak. Correct any misalignment by adjusting the tongue-and-groove joint slightly with each row. You can also snap additional control lines to help align the rows.

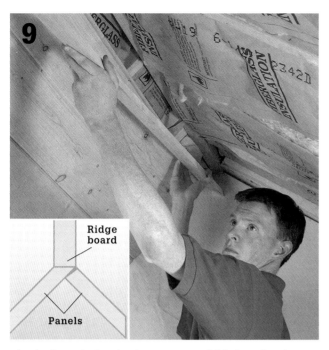

9

10

Rip the boards for the last row to width, beveling the top edges so they fit flush against the ridge board. Facenail the boards in place. Install paneling on the other side of the ceiling, then cut and install the final row of panels to form a closed joint under the ridge board (inset).

Install trim molding along walls, at joints around obstacles, and along inside and outside corners, if desired. (Select-grade 1 × 2 works well as trim along walls.) Where necessary, bevel the back edges of the trim or miter-cut the ends to accommodate the slope of the ceiling.

Tips for Paneling an Attic Ceiling ▸

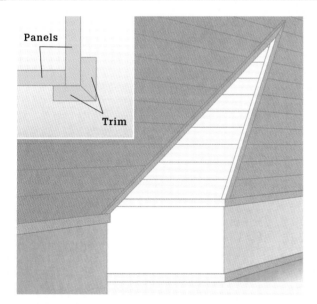

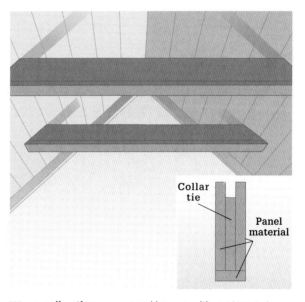

Use mitered trim to cover joints where panels meet at outside corners. Dormers and other roof elements create opposing ceiling angles that can be difficult to panel around. It may be easier to butt the panels together and hide the butt joints with custom-cut trim. The trim also makes a nice transition between angles.

Wrap collar ties or exposed beams with custom-cut panels. Install the paneling on the ceiling first. Then, rip-cut panels to the desired width. You may want to include a tongue-and-groove joint as part of the trim detail. Angle-cut the ends of the trim so it fits tight to the ceiling panels.

24. Installing Ceiling Beams

Installing ceiling beams adds depth and visual appeal to vaulted or high ceilings, or even regular 8-ft. ceilings that are a bit on the bland side. The beams of this project are purely decorative, but meant to suggest the heavy-duty structural members of timber-frame construction. Choose a higher-grade lumber for a cleaner look, or a lower grade for a more rustic approach. The species of wood you use to build the beams may match your existing trimwork, although clear-coated hardwood beams will be more expensive than paint-grade counterparts.

Whenever possible, install ceiling beams with fasteners driven into blocking or joists. Installation of ceiling beams is not recommended without solid backing. Standard wallboard construction is not built to hold the weight of this project with hollow wall fasteners and construction adhesive alone. Use hollow wall fasteners only when absolutely necessary.

Tools & Materials ▸

Pencil	1 × 6 and
Tape measure	1 × 4 boards
Circular saw with	2 × 6 framing
straightedge guide	lumber
Power miter saw	Cove moldings
Drill with bits	3" Wallboard screws
Pneumatic finish-	Construction
nail gun and	adhesive
compressor	Hollow wall
Caulk gun	fasteners
Combination square	1¼" pneumatic
Painter's tape	finish nails
Chalk line	Wood glue

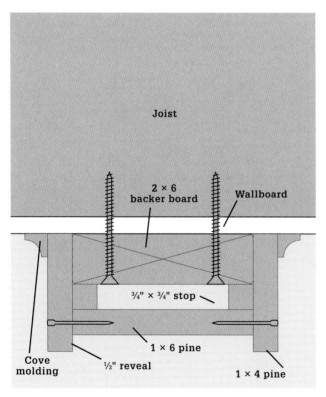

A cross-section view of the exposed beams shown being installed here reveals that they are hollow inside and actually quite simple in structure. You can install beams in any direction, but perpendicular to the ceiling joists (as shown above) is the easier orientation to work with.

Exposed beams lend a feeling of strength and structure to a room, even if they're really just hollow shells like the beams seen here. Because they can be attached directly to the ceiling surface, installing decorative beams is a relatively easy trim carpentry project (as long as you're comfortable working at heights).

How to Install Ceiling Beams

1

Plan the approximate location of each ceiling beam and locate the ceiling joists in the desired areas with a stud finder. Mark the joists on the ceiling with tape.

2

Mark the end of each joist at the point where the ceiling meets the wall. If you will be installing the beams parallel to the joists, as shown here, measure out from the center of each joist one-half the width of the backer board you'll be installing (2¾" for a 2 × 6) and make a reference mark. Make reference marks at the same relative spots where the opposite wall meets the ceiling. For installations parallel to the joists, offsetting the marks results in visible reference lines for the edges of the backer boards.

3

Use a chalk line to snap straight reference lines across the ceiling. Have a helper hold the line on the corresponding reference mark. If you are installing the beams perpendicular to the joists, you may want to avoid snapping a chalk line, since marking chalk (especially red chalk) is hard to remove and can even telegraph through paint. An option that won't mark up the ceiling is to string a grid of unchalked lines across the ceiling to mark the positions of the beams and the locations of the joists. Then, mark an X at every point where the lines intersect and remove the lines before installing the backer boards for the beams.

(continued)

4

Reference line

Measure, cut, and install 2 × 6 backer boards according to your reference lines. Use construction adhesive to adhere the blocking to the ceiling and drive 3" wallboard screws through the blocking and into the joists. *Tip: If you're working alone, drive a few screws into the backers (preferably at known joist locations) before you position it. Then, you can hold the board in place with one hand and drive the screws with the other hand. A better plan, of course, is to recruit a helper.*

Option: In areas where a ceiling joist is not available and blocking is difficult to install, use hollow wall fasteners (such as the toggle bolt shown here) to install the backers. At the end of each backer you can drive 3" screws toenail style into the top plate of the wall to provide additional support.

5

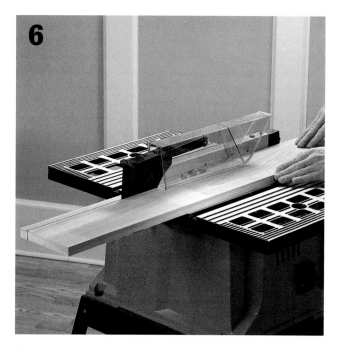

6

Set the blade of a combination square to 1¼" and mark the back face of the 1 × 4 beam sides with a pencil. Slide the square along the edge of the piece and hold the tip of the pencil against the end of the blade. Mark enough stock for each beam side.

Use a table saw (best tool) or a circular saw and a straightedge guide to cut ¾" × ¾" strips off of pine for the stop molding. Cut enough stock to apply to each beam side piece.

7

Align the stop-molding strips with the reference marks on the beam sides. Nail and glue the ¾" strips to the back faces of the beam sides with 1¼" finish nails and wood glue.

8

Cut the side pieces to length with a power miter saw, using scarf joints to join each piece that is more then 8 ft. long. Butt the ends of the beams into the opposing walls, making sure the joints are tight. Nail the sides in place using 1½" finish nails driven every 12" into the blocking.

9

Install the bottom pieces of the beams with wood glue and 1½" nails driven into the ¾" strips on the inside of the beams. Make sure the ends butt into the walls snugly, and use scarf joints where joining pieces together (offset the scarf joints from seams in the beam sides).

10

Install cove molding along the seam between the beams and the ceiling with 1¼" finish nails. Drive the nails into the sides of the beams. Apply the finish of your choice to the beams, filling the nail holes appropriately.

APPENDIX: Cutting & Fitting Joints

Cutting and fitting joints is a skill that requires patience, knowledge, and well-maintained equipment to achieve effective results. There are a few basic joints that are generally used for most trim applications: butt, inside and outside miter, scarf, and coped joints.

Although cutting trim joints accurately is the key function of a power miter saw, it is not the only tool necessary for quality joinery. Coped joints require a coping saw as well as a set of metal files. For some trim applications such as frame and panel wainscoting, fitting butt joints is simplified with the use of a biscuit jointer or a pocket hole jig. These are specialty tools designed for joining wood.

Cutting and fitting joints during installation can be very frustrating, especially when it involves difficult walls that are not plumb and corners that are out of square. Take the time to read through the proper techniques of using a miter saw, as well as the correct method for cutting each individual joint. These techniques are described in detail to help you work through the imperfections found in every house and avoid common problems during installation.

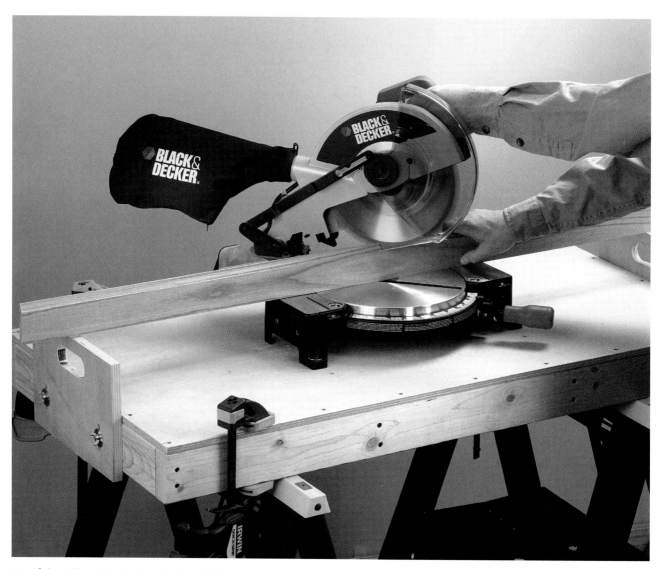

Careful cutting is the hallmark of good joinery, be it in making furniture or installing trim moldings. Used correctly, a power miter saw offers the speed and precision to make your project look like it was done by a pro.

Power Miter Saw Techniques

There are two main types of power miter saws. The basic style cuts mitered angles when material is placed against the fence or beveled angles when material is placed flat on the work surface. The second type is called a compound miter saw. Compound saws allow you to cut a miter and a bevel simultaneously. The compound angle is extremely helpful in situations where a corner is out of plumb and a mitered angle requires a bevel to compensate. Some compound saws are available with a sliding feature that allows you to cut through wider stock with a smaller blade size. This option raises the cost of the saw considerably.

Creep cuts. To avoid cutting off too much, start out by making a cut about ¼" to the waste side of the cutting line, then nibble at the workpiece with one or more additional cuts until you have cut up to the cutting line. Wait until the blade stops before raising the arm on every cut.

How to Make Repeat Cuts

To cut multiple pieces of stock to the same length, clamp a stop block to your support table at the desired distance from the blade. After cutting the first piece, position each additional length against the stop block and the fence to cut pieces of equal length.

How to Cut Wide Stock

With a power miter saw: Make a full downward cut. Release the trigger and let the blade come to a full stop, then raise the saw arm. Flip the workpiece over and finish the cut

With a Sliding Compound Miter Saw: Equipped with a saw carriage that slides away from the fence, these saws have greater cutting capacity than a nonsliding saw so they can cut wider stock. They're also more expensive, but you may find it worth renting one.

Mitering Outside Corners

Cutting outside miters is one of the main functions of a power miter saw. Most saws have positive stops (called detents) at 45° in each direction, so standard outside corners are practically cut for you by the saw. Keep in mind that your saw must be accurately set up to cut joints squarely. Read the owner's manual for setting up your saw as well as for safety precautions. Before you begin, check the walls for square with a combination square or a framing square. If the corner is very close to square, proceed with the square corner installation. If the corner is badly out of square, follow the "Out of Square" procedure on the following page.

Tools & Materials ▸

Combination square or framing square	Air compressor
	Air hose
Miter saw	T-bevel
Pencil	Molding
Tape measure	Masking tape
Pneumatic finish nail gun	1 × 4

How To Miter Square Outside Corners

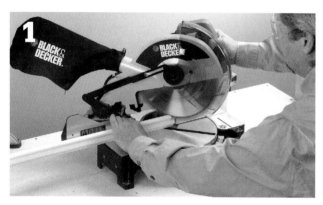

Set the miter saw to 45°. Position the first piece on-edge, flat on the miter box table, flush against the fence. Hold the piece firmly in place with your left hand and cut the trim with a slow, steady motion. Release the power button of the saw and remove the molding after the blade stops.

Set the miter saw blade to the opposing 45° positive stop. Place the second piece of molding on-edge, flat on the saw table, flush against the fence. Fasten the piece tightly in place with a hold-down or clamp. Cut the molding with a slow, steady motion.

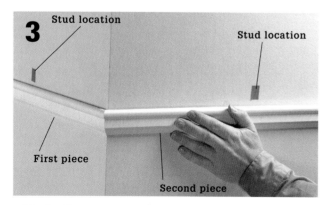

With the first piece of molding tacked in place, hold the second piece in position and check the fit of the joint. If the joint is tight, nail both pieces at stud locations.

If the corner joint does not fit tightly, shim the work piece away from the fence to make minor adjustments until the joint fits tightly. Shims should be a uniform thickness. Playing cards work well.

How to Miter Out-of-Square Outside Corners

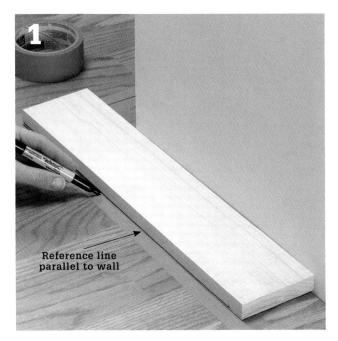

Draw a reference line off each wall of the corner using a straight 1 × 4. Put masking tape down on the finished floor to avoid scuffing it and to see your lines clearly. Trace along each wall, connecting the traced lines at a point out from the tip of the corner.

To find the angle you need to miter your moldings, place a T-bevel with the handle flush against one wall, and adjust the blade so that it intersects the point where your reference lines meet. Lock the blade in place at this angle.

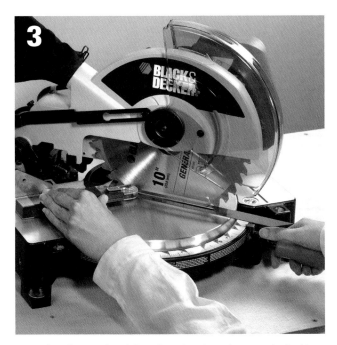

Transfer the angle of the T-bevel to the miter saw by locking the saw in the down position and adjusting the angle to match the angle of the T-bevel.

Position the molding on-edge, flat on the saw table and flush against the fence. Cut at your cutting mark. Tack the workpiece in place and repeat steps 2 through 4 to measure and cut the mating piece. Or, you can subtract the angle of the first cut (for example, 47°) from 90° to find the angle for the second cut (43° in this case). Using math is faster; taking direct measurements is more reliable.

Mitering Inside Corners

Although most professionals prefer to cope-cut inside corners, it is common to see moldings that are mitered to inside corners. These joints are more likely to separate over time and to allow gaps to show. For that reason it is not advised to use inside corner miters when installing a stain-grade trim product. The gaps will be visible and are very difficult to fill with putty. For paint-grade projects, mitering inside corners makes more sense because joints can be filled and sanded before the top coats of paint are applied.

Tools & Materials ▸

Miter saw
Pencil
Tape measure
Utility knife
Pneumatic finish nail gun
Air compressor
Air hose
Molding

How To Miter Square Inside Corners

Set the miter saw to 45° and place the first piece of trim on-edge, flat on the miter box table and flush against the fence. Hold the piece firmly in place with your left hand and cut the trim with a slow, steady motion. Release the power button and remove the molding after the blade stops.

Back-cut the inside edge of the trim piece with a utility knife so that the top corner will sit flush against the wall corner.

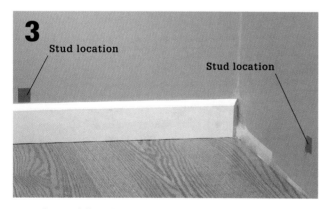

Butt the molding tightly against the wallboard and tack it into place.

Adjust the blade of the miter saw to the opposite 45° angle and cut the mating piece. Test the fit of the joint, adjusting the miter angle if necessary. Once the fit is tight, nail both pieces at stud locations.

Out-of-Plumb Corner Cuts

Out-of-plumb walls are concave, convex, or simply not perpendicular to the floor and ceiling at one or more points. It is a common condition. In some cases, the condition is caused by the fact that wallboard sheets have tapered edges to make taping joints easier and the tapers fall at the edge of a work area where trim is installed. In other cases, the condition may be caused by wall framing issues. In either case, you'll find that it's easier to adapt your trim pieces to the wall than to try and straighten out the finished wall surface. To do this, the trim pieces need to be cut to match the out-of-plumb area, to compensate for the taper in the panel. Another option is to install a running spacer along the bottom edge and cut your molding square, as on the previous page.

How to Make Out-of-Plumb Corner Cuts

1

Stud location

Stud location

Place a T-bevel into the corner and press the blade flush to the wall surface. Tighten the adjustment knob so the blade conforms to the angle of the profile of the wall.

2

Transfer the angle of the T-bevel to the miter saw blade by locking the saw in the down position and adjusting the angle to match the angle of the T-bevel. Cut the molding to match the angle.

Tip ▶

Bevel gauge

Occasionally, a compound cut is necessary for cutting miters on out-of-plumb corners. When this situation arises, set the bevel of the miter saw to match the out-of-plumb wall (inset photo) and miter the angle at the appropriate degree. Compound cuts can be difficult to get right the first time, so test the fit with a piece of scrap material first.

Making Coped Cuts

At first glance, coping moldings appears to be difficult work that only a professional would attempt. But, in actuality, coping only requires patience and the right tools. Whether a molding is installed flat against the wall, or is sprung to fill an inside corner junction, as with crown molding, the concept of coping is the same. It is essentially cutting back the body of a trim piece along its profile. This cutting is done at an angle so that only the face of the molding makes direct contact with the adjoining piece.

For beginners, coping a molding requires a coping saw, a utility knife, and a set of metal files with a variety of profiles. The initial cope cut is made with the coping saw and the joint is fitted with a utility knife and files. This fitting can be a long process, especially when working with intricate crown moldings, but the end results are superior to any other method.

Tools & Materials ▸

Miter saw	Pneumatic finish
Metal files or rasp set	nail gun
Utility knife	Air compressor
Pencil	Air hose
Tape measure	Molding

Coping is a tricky skill to learn, but a valuable capability to possess once you've got the process down. With very few exceptions, a coped cut can be made only with a hand saw (usually, a coping saw like the one shown in the photo above).

How to Cope-Cut Moldings

1

Measure, cut, and install the first trim piece. Square-cut the ends, butting them tightly into the corners, and nail the workpiece at the marked stud locations.

Cut the second piece of molding at a 45° angle as if it were an inside miter. The cut edge reveals the profile of the cope cut.

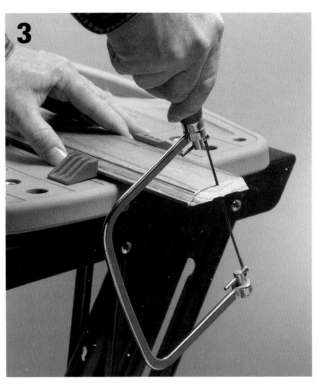

Starting with the most delicate edge of the molding, cut along the front edge of the molding with a coping saw, following the contour exactly. Bevel the cut at 45° to create a sharp edge along the contour.

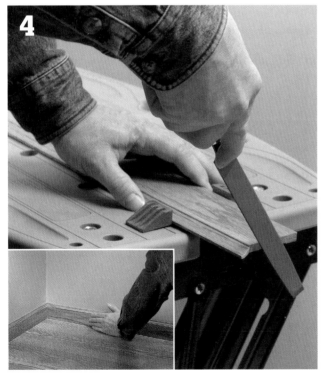

Test-fit the piece (inset photo) and use a metal file to fit the joint precisely. When the joint is properly fitted, nail the coped piece in place.

Tip ▶

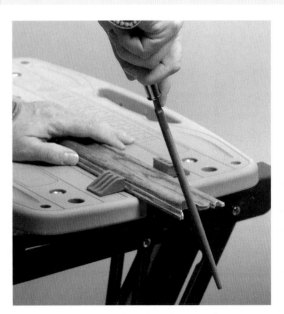

Trim components such as this chair rail can be complex to cope properly. A variety of rasps or metal files with different profiles is the key to fitting these joints tightly.

Cutting Mitered Returns

Mitered returns are a decorative treatment used to hide the end grain of wood and provide a finished appearance when molding stops prior to the end of a wall. Mitered returns range from tiny pieces of base shoe up to very large crown moldings. They are also commonly used when installing a stool and apron treatment or on decorative friezes above doors.

Bevel returns are another simple return option for chair rails, baseboards, and base shoe. A bevel return is simply a cut at the end of the molding that "returns" the workpiece back to the wall at an angle. The biggest advantage to using mitered returns rather than bevel returns is that mitered returns already have a finish applied. Bevel returns require more touchups.

Cutting mitered returns for small moldings, such as quarter round, or for thin stock, such as baseboard, can be tricky when using a power miter saw. The final cut of the process leaves the return loose where it can sometimes be thrown from the saw due to the air current of the blade. Plan on using a piece of trim that is long enough to cut comfortably, or you will find yourself fighting the saw.

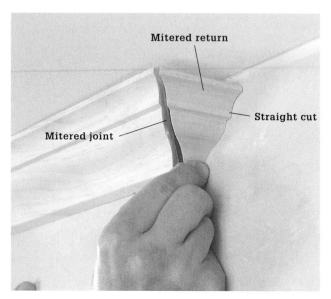

Mitered returns finish molding ends that would otherwise be exposed. Miter the main piece as you would at an outside corner. Cut a miter on the return piece, then cut it to length with a straight cut so it butts to the wall. Attach the return piece with wood glue.

Tools & Materials ▸

Combination square
Utility knife
Power miter saw

Miter box and back saw
Pencil
Tape measure

Pneumatic finish nail gun
Air compressor
Air hose

T-bevel
Molding
Wood glue

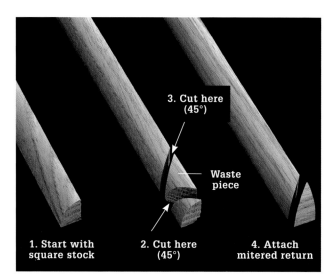

Returns are made from two 45° angle cuts. The scrap piece is removed and the return piece is glued into place.

How to Cut Mitered Base Shoe Returns

Measure and mark the molding to length. Adjust the miter saw blade to 45° and back-miter the molding, cutting the front edge to the desired overall length of the trim. Nail the back-mitered piece in place using a square to line it up flush with the edge of the door casing.

Adjust the blade of the miter saw to the opposite 45° angle and miter-cut the molding using a slow, steady stroke.

Hold the mitered molding against the baseboard at a right angle above the installed base shoe. Mark the molding at the depth of the installed base shoe. Square-cut the molding at the cutoff mark. Because making this cut with a power saw is very dangerous, use a miter box and a back saw. The cut-off piece will be the mitered return piece.

Mitered return

Check the fit of the return against the baseboard. If it is too small repeat steps 3 and 4, making the piece slightly larger. If the return is too large, trim it to fit with a utility knife or sandpaper. Once the return fits properly, glue it in place with wood glue.

Beveled return

Option: Beveled returns are a quick and simple alternative to mitered returns. They require finish touchup after the trim is installed.

Creative Publishing
international

Copyright © 2010
Creative Publishing international, Inc.
400 First Avenue North, Suite 300
Minneapolis, Minnesota 55401
1-800-328-0590
www.creativepub.com
All rights reserved

Printed at R. R. Donnelley

10 9 8 7 6 5 4 3 2 1

President/CEO: Ken Fund
VP for Sales & Marketing: Kevin Hamric

Home Improvement Group

Publisher: Bryan Trandem
Managing Editor: Tracy Stanley
Senior Editor: Mark Johanson
Editor: Jennifer Gehlhar

Creative Director: Michele Lanci-Altomare
Senior Design Managers: Jon Simpson, Brad Springer
Design Manager: James Kegley

Lead Photographer: Joel Schnell

Production Managers: Linda Halls, Laura Hokkanen

Page Layout Artist: Danielle Smith

Here's How: Trimwork
Created by: The Editors of Creative Publishing international, Inc., in cooperation with Black & Decker. Black & Decker® is a trademark of The Black & Decker Corporation and is used under license.